The 13 Commandments Of Haunting

The 13 Commandments Of Haunting

By Scott Swenson
Edited By Philip Hernandez

This is a work of creative nonfiction. Some parts have been fictionalized in varying degrees, for various purposes.

Copyright © 2020 by Philip L. Hernandez
Cover Illustration Copyright © 2020 by Scott Swenson

All rights reserved. No part of this book may be reproduced or used in any manner without written permission of the copyright owner except for the use of quotations in a book review.
For more information, address: hernandez.philip@gmail.com.

First paperback edition November 2020

Cover Illustration by Scott Swenson

ISBN 978-1-7332733-2-9 (paperback)
ISBN 978-1-7332733-3-6 (ebook)

Published by Philip Hernandez
www.philiplhernandez.com

TABLE OF CONTENTS

INTRODUCTION.. 1

PART ONE – Philosophy: How to Think Like a Haunter 3

   CHAPTER 1: A Haunt Is a Theater You Walk Through 5

      Get Involved with Your Local Theater to Make
Great Connections.. 6

      Need Actors? 6

      To Learn about Actors, Audition for a Role 7

      Connect with Marketing Folks 7

      Become a Scenic Painter or a Special-Effects
Person for Theater... 8

      Keep Your Haunt in the Public Eye All Year Round 9

      Learn from Theater Directors 10

      Don't Be Afraid to Share 11

      Haunts and Theaters Source Much of the Same Stuff 12

      Sponsor One Another 13

      Do a Cool Fundraiser Together 13

   CHAPTER 2: A Haunt Might Be Seasonal, but Haunting Is
Year-Round Work... 15

      Start the Year by Planning for Your Halloween Haunt 15

      Figure Out Your Story and Your Storage 16

Shopping for Your Haunted Attraction Year-Round 17
   Christmas 17
      Projector Lights 18
      Battery-powered Lighting 18
      Tricks with Fake Trees 19
      Remote-controlled Outlets 20
      Spray Snow 20
      An Aside: Thoughts on Christmas Haunts 20
   Valentine's Day 21
   St. Patrick's Day 22
   Easter 22
   Fourth of July 24
Summer—The Time to Prepare for the Halloween Season 24
   The Importance of Auditions 24
   Start Your Marketing Campaign 26
   Your Best Marketing Resource 27
   Look for Partners and Sponsors 27
   The Build 28
   Document the Good, the Bad, and the Ugly 29
Keep Your Eyes Open All Year Round for Bargains 30
Finding the Unusual on Vacation 31
Always Have Your Camera with You 31

CHAPTER 3: Criticism Is a Gift 33
   Three Steps for Processing Criticism 35
   Assess Which Criticism Is Valid and Which Isn't 36
   Listen to Guests as They Exit Your Haunt 37
   Survey Your Guests, and Respond to Criticism 37
   Guests Want to Know They've Been Heard 39
   What to Do When Other Attractions Post Negative
   Comments about Your Haunt 40

Table of Contents

Be Kind to Your Competitors—It Only Benefits You 42
Healthy Competition Helps the Industry and
Helps Your Haunt 43
Collaborate with Other Haunts on Advertising and Tickets 45
Go Enjoy Other People's Haunts, and Get Inspired 45

CHAPTER 4: The Haunt Director's Role Is to Magnify
Not to Shine 47
The Director Is the Lens, Not the Sun 47
A Good Director Makes Every Else's Work Look Better 48
The Director Takes Responsibility for Live Performers 48
Casting—Putting the Right People in the Right Jobs 49
Working with Designers 52
Training Actors 53
    Give the Actor Ownership of Their Character 54
    Ask Questions to Help Them Learn about Their Character 54
    Keep Actors from Going Rogue 57
The Magic of Positive Reinforcement 58
    Praise People Publicly, Redirect Them Privately 58
Model the Behavior You Want to See 59

CHAPTER 5: Choose Your Level of Extreme Early 61
How to Determine What's Too Much 61
Should You Allow Performers to Touch Guests? 62
Is It Revolutionary, or Is It Gimmicky? 64
Is It Storytelling, or Is It Just Shock for Shock's Sake? 65
Understand Your Audience, and Have Appropriate Sensitivity 66
How about an R-rated Haunt? 68
How Far to Go with Torture 69
How to Do Blood Effectively 69
Limits in Escape Rooms 70
Make Sure Whatever You Do Fits the Story 71
Market Your Haunt so Guests Know What to Expect 72

CHAPTER 6: The Four Levels of Haunt—the Importance of Targeting One of the Four Demographic Audiences 75
    The Four Haunt Audiences.. 75
    Halloween Events for Kids 76
        Dress-up and Pretend.. 77
        Have Something for the Older Siblings 78
        Don't Go Totally Dark 78
        A Haybale Adventure 79
    Halloween Events for Tweens 79
        Ghosts—Yes. Gore—Not So Much.. 80
        How About Z-tag? 80
    Halloween Events for Teens-plus... 81
        Deliver the Unexpected.. 81
    Halloween Events for Adults 82
        This Group Wants Psychological Fear....................................... 82
        Include Food and Cocktails... 83
    Decide on Your Target Audience, and Commit to It 83
    What about No-scare Amulets and Lights-on Nights?................ 84
        Instead, Ramp Up the Fear 85

PART TWO – Guts and Bolts: Operations 101............................ 87
    CHAPTER 7: Set Your Direction, and Communicate It 89
    The Challenge... 89
    Determine Your Goals, and Learn How to Translate Them........ 90
    Emphasize the Importance of Collaboration.................................. 91
    Set Good Groundwork to Create Win-Win Scenarios................ 92
    Chris Kleckner on Communication... 92
        Adjectives, Research, and Collaboration 94
        Use Science to Create Fantasy 96
        Bad Ideas Often Spark Great Ideas.. 97

The Event Brainstormer—an Invaluable Tool for
Generating Ideas 98

CHAPTER 8: Sound Makes a Difference 101
Sound Is Essential to Bring Guests Completely into
Your World 101
Sound Makes a Space Seem Larger and Enhances the Scares 102
Audio Turns Your Haunt into a Horror Film.............................. 103
    Create an Underscore.. 104
    Use Sound to Heighten Suspense 105
Use Point-Source Audio to Draw Guests' Attention 106
    Point-Source Audio Enhances the Realism......................... 107
Audio Equipment Doesn't Need to Be Expensive 108
Design Your Haunt for the Equipment You Have 108
Work with Your Local University 109
The Value of Triggers.. 110
Sources of Great Haunt Sounds 111
Sources of Live and Recorded Music and Sound Effects........... 112

CHAPTER 9: Auditions—and How to Survive Them 115
Auditions Get People Talking about Your Haunt Months
Before Halloween... 116
Everything an Actor Does Is Part of the Audition 116
If You're Asked to Prepare, Prepare!.. 117
Show Up on Time... 119
Advice for Haunt Owners and Casting Directors 120
Everybody Wants You to Have a Great Audition 121
The Audition Isn't Over when It's Over 122
Don't Stay in Character after the Audition Is Over, and
Forgetthe Gimmicks... 123
Follow Up in a Professional Way 124

CHAPTER 10: Actors Require Care and Feeding 127
    Know What You're Looking For 128
    Consider Double Casting 129
    Every Performer Needs Compensation, but that Doesn't
    Have to Be Money 130
    Don't Ignore the Small Print 131
    "Where Can I Find Haunt Actors, and How Can They
    Find Me?" 132
    You're Not Necessarily Looking for "Actors" 133
    Why Auditions Are Essential 135
        Audition by Doing 135
        The Four Things to Look for in an Audition 136
        Games to Use at Auditions 137
    Training Your Actors 138
        Teach Your Actors to Read Guests 140
    Retain Your Actors by Catching Them Doing Things Right 140

CHAPTER 11: Make It Good, Make It Fast, or Make It Cheap—
Pick Two 143
    Tricks Used in Famous Movies 144
    Creating Affordable Scenery—Reuse, Repaint,
    and Repurpose 145
        Use What's Already There 147
        Exchange Sweat Equity for Free Materials 147
    Great Sources for Costumes 148
        Fun with Great Stuff™, Sobo Fabric Glue,
        and Cheese Graters 149
    Clever Ideas for Inexpensive Masks and Manikins 150
    Super Cheap Makeup Ideas 151
        New Uses for Common Foods 153
    Terrific Blood Recipes 154

Finding Free Props 155
The Importance of Investing in Hero Props............................. 156

PART THREE – The Haunt Community 157

CHAPTER 12: The Pros and Cons of Shows and Cons 159
Three Excellent Events for Haunters to Attend......................... 159
Seasonal Entertainment Source Leadership Symposium....... 159
Midsummer Scream 160
Urban Death 161
"Why Should I Go?"... 161
You'll Be the First to Know about New Haunt Products 163
Network, Network, Network... 163
Take Plenty of Photos 165
Attend Parties.. 165
Don't Forget Your Credit Card... 165
Review the Contacts You Made 166
The Advantages of Attending a Parallel Industry Tradeshow........ 166
Be Present When You're There.. 167
A Seminar on First Impressions Confirms My Views 168
Presenting and Serving Food that Integrates with
the Event Theme 169
A Different Photo Op and Other Unique Ideas for Haunts..... 169
A Seminar on Storytelling 170
What's Old Is New—in a Different Venue 171
A Virtual-Reality Dining Experience
and Other Discoveries... 172
Keep Your Eyes, Ears, and Mind Open 174
A Great Opportunity to Share Information
with Professionals in AnotherArea 174
"Is It Worth It?" 175
The Big Question—Which Show to Attend 176

Chapter 13: When the Blood Flows, All Haunts Rise 179
  Stop the Trash Talk 179
  Not Only Does Your Reputation Suffer, So Does
  the Industry 180
  So, You Want to Be a Full-time Haunter. 181
  If You're Looking for Work, Be Someone Who Fits
  with the Culture 182
  Speak Up Against Negativity 183
  Find Reasons to Compliment Rather than Complain ... 184
  Think about Multi-Event Tickets 185

Final Words 187

References 189

About the Publisher 191

About the Author 193

Introduction

Throughout my college years, I attended some of the coolest parties filled with an incredibly diverse cast of characters. We'd have discussions that became more elevated and impactful as the night wore on. I'm sure some of that was due to the ongoing consumption of alcohol, but most of it came from embracing the moment and allowing the conversations and revelations to build upon themselves. It was the power of the spoken word. On mornings after these parties, I'd wonder, "How did we ever come up with that stuff?" or, more often, "What did we say exactly?" The process of assembling this book was very similar to those "mornings after."

Let me clarify. The content you're about to consume comes from episodes of my podcast, "A Scott in the Dark." The book's editor, Philip Hernandez, transcribed the first 30 episodes and released them as blog posts. This book contains the 13 most popular (best trending) of those episodes.

When I write a podcast episode, I do it in outline form, and then I just talk, using the outline to keep from going too far off track. (If you've listened to the show, you know I'm not always successful in this endeavor.) As I read through the content of this book, I was excited to find that so much of my "off the cuff" information is actually helpful. I'm also grateful that Philip has helped sand off some of the rough edges while maintaining the original playfulness and spontaneity. He makes me sound a lot smarter than I really am!

Not only has Philip captured the content, he's arranged it all into cohesive groupings. This means you can either read the book from cover to cover OR you can pick and choose chapters based on your current need.

It's also important to note that many of these podcasts were recorded prior to COVID-19 and the changing operational practices that followed. I still believe that the vast majority of this information is applicable. Please take the evergreen theories presented here and apply the appropriate post-pandemic filter.

I'm very proud of this book, and I truly hope you enjoy reading it. If you can take away even one piece of beneficial information, I'll consider it a success.

If I could go back in time, I'd invite Philip to all of those cool parties. Who knows what information we'd have today???

- Scott Swenson

PART ONE

PHILOSOPHY: HOW TO THINK LIKE A PROFESSIONAL HAUNTER

Chapter 1

A Haunt Is Theater You Walk Through

Theater and haunt can work together in ways you may not have thought of before. For those of you who've listened to my podcasts, read my blogs, met me, or seen any of my presentations at various and sundry shows, you know I believe haunt and theater are the same thing. Haunted attractions are a theater piece that you walk through. I've always believed that, and I'll continue to believe that. This doesn't mean you, as a haunter, have to be remarkably well versed in theater, but it's important to understand the basics.

Almost every community has some sort of local theater scene. I've done a lot of stuff with an organization in Tampa called Theater Tampa Bay—everything from judging productions to sitting on the board. If you're not involved in your local theater, you might want to branch out a little.

What I'm going to talk about in this chapter is why and how theater can benefit you as a haunter. You have to begin by accepting that haunt is theater. You may think you're a haunter, not a theater person, but they're so interrelated. Haunters can learn a lot from the theater community, and the theater community can benefit from the experience haunters bring. So, it's a win-win scenario when you get involved with your local theater company.

Get Involved with Your Local Theater to Make Great Connections

The first benefit that comes to mind when you start involving yourself with your local theater community is you make some great connections. You meet some wonderful people that can benefit you as a haunter—lighting designers, audio designers, and so forth. These people may have a freak flag they want to fly every now and then, and what better way to do that than designing lighting or sound for a haunted attraction? They can bring a whole different perspective and a whole different emotional language to your haunt. The best way to get to know these people is to work with them, so get out there and volunteer at your local community theater or find a professional theater that needs some extra help—and that's almost any theater.

You may feel you have absolutely no experience, but, as a haunter, you have experience with everything from hanging lights to hiding cords to recording music and sound effects to installing speakers to building sets to distressing things to making costumes to doing makeup. You've definitely got some experience and, if you find the right theater company, you'll be able to edge your way in and start making those connections.

Need Actors?

Not only do theater companies provide a great opportunity to meet designers, they're great places to recruit actors. I'm aware there's an ongoing debate about this. I've heard haunters say, "I don't hire actors, because they don't know how to haunt." My feeling is you've hired the wrong actors, because good actors—trained actors—can adapt to the situation of a haunt. I've done it, and I know it works. The trick is to get people who don't think they're actors but are actory, if you know what I mean. If you get people who are really good actors and can create wonderful characters, they can bring a whole new life to your queue line and your key moments in the storytelling process. Plus, they may be able to connect you with folks who may not be trained stage actors but might be absolutely perfect for your haunt. So, again, your local theater is a great way to connect with actors and even staff.

If you're a haunt actor, I strongly recommend you audition for some form of theater if you haven't already. Even if it's a community theater and a volunteer situation, you'll learn so much about how to affect people emotionally, how to make it fresh each night, how to reinvent the same thing over and over and over so every single guest experiences it like it's the first time you've ever done it. It gives your acting chops off-season polish when you do that.

To Learn About Actors, Audition for a Role

If you're interested in being an actor in a piece of live theater, audition for a role. Whether you get the job or not, it will give you a better understanding of the vibe at auditions. If you happen to be a casting director at a haunt, for example, audition for a role. This is a great way to get a feeling for how nervous those actors are, and you'll also understand the importance of finding the right people for the right role. In addition, going through a theater audition may give you some new ideas on how to find people who can do exactly what you need them to do for your haunt.

Connect with Marketing Folks

Other good connections you might make in doing local theater—whether it's professional or community—is with their marketing folks. Find out how they market their plays. Do they use social media? Do they contact local news folk? Do they try to get on the radio? You might find something you hadn't thought about. Theater companies are running on the same shoestring budgets as haunted attractions. Most of them are nonprofit organizations, whether they're professional or not, and they get grant money, but they're still trying to make every dollar spend like $10, $20, or

$30. So, hang out with their marketing folks, find out what connections they have. Find a way to share databases (yours and theirs), because there's an overlap among haunt fans and theater fans. You might be able to really expand both your databases.

Don't be afraid to volunteer. Everybody thinks, "I can't give anything away," but, the truth is, you're not giving anything away. You're investing in your product by helping somebody else out, so, come haunt season, they might say, "Here's our list of who we contact when we open a new show." If you're really lucky, somebody will say, "Here's our donor list," or, "Here's our board list." These are people who are already interested in supporting some sort of performance, and they just might, around Halloween time, want to help out something spooky. So that's another reason to get into the theater and make those connections.

Become a Scenic Painter or Special-Effects Person for Theater

Of equal importance to the connections you might make is the experience. If you're a haunter who's fascinated with building sets, the more sets you get to build and the more scenic painting you do, the better you get at it. The way a lot of theater companies work is they have a set designer who designs the set and is usually the lead construction guy or gal as well. They're always looking for scenic painters—people who can come in and make the walls they've built look like rich oak paneling or metal or wallpaper or anything but what the walls are actually made of.

Does all of this sound familiar? If you've ever done a haunted attraction, chances are good you've done some form of scenic painting and had to make a plain plywood wall look like it belonged in a gothic manor or inside a factory or the interior of a spaceship. Building scenic for haunted attractions is no different than building scenic for theaters. Professional theaters and even community theaters will sometimes pay people to do this, so it can be a way to earn a little extra money while gaining additional experience for your haunt.

The other thing that theaters are always looking for—depending on the production, of course—is people who can do some type of special effects. Even if you haven't done specifically what they need, I'm sure you could help. You could make suggestions about situations in which they could use monofilament or a spring trap or pneumatics or anything and everything we use in haunts all the time. Obviously, not every piece of theater requires this, but there are shows like Dracula, Rocky Horror Picture Show, the musical Jekyll and Hyde, and Blithe Spirit that have different needs for special effects.

If you're a makeup artist or a costume designer in a haunt, you can use those skills in live theater, so why not get paid for them? Why not put together a portfolio of costumes that don't have blood on them, things that aren't covered in Great Stuff™, and some of your 18th-century Edwardian Steam Punk Goth material? Get the blood off, take the watch gears off, and now you've got costumes for The Importance of Being Earnest, if you so desire. That's another great opportunity to get paid while you're refining and adding to your skills.

Keep Your Haunt in the Public Eye All Year Round

The other thing that working with your local theater does—whether you're an actor, a designer, or whatever you do for your haunt—is give you something to put on your haunt's website: "Come see John and Marsha So-and-So in Such-and-Such play, and then come see us in October." It's a way to remain in touch with your haunt audience, because you're constantly giving them other things to do. It gives you an opportunity to build a following online—"Go see Bill So-and-So's lighting at the Such-and-Such community theater." It keeps you viable, it makes you visible within the community, and it builds your credibility. When your haunt comes around, somebody might think, "Oh yeah, I saw those actors in the Odd Couple. They were hysterical. I wonder if they can be scary." Well, yes, they can!

Working in your community theater keeps your haunt, your haunt actors, and your haunt designers in the public eye, even in the off season. Also, if you're a haunt actor, it gives you the opportunity to perhaps be seen by haunt owners. Invite them to come and see your show, so when the haunt season rolls around, you're on the top of their list. Or maybe they'll write something specifically for you. I've done this many, many times. The haunt owner or director will know, when going into casting, that they want to see a particular actor at the audition, because they've written a piece with them in mind. You've heard me talk about one of my dearest friends, the great haunt actress Luna Mystique AKA Diana Bennett. I've written roles specifically for her many times, because I know what she can do, and it makes my job as a casting director so much easier.

If you're an actor and you haven't built up much of a rapport with haunt owners, or you're in a new town or environment, get involved with the local theater, even if your end goal is to work as a haunter. You can invite the haunt owners to come and see you. They may or may not come, but they know you're an actor, and they know you're interested.

If you're a smart haunt owner, you'll go to some of your local theater productions—even high school and college theater productions—to see who's out there as far as talent goes. Sometimes, actors don't even think about haunted attractions as an option. Some of them don't want to do it, and that's fine. If they don't want to do it, you don't want them. But others may not even realize it's an option, and they'll think, "I'd be able to act, and I might get some money for it!" If you're a volunteer haunt, these actors may want to do what they love to do just for some sort of recognition or a coupon to McDonald's. Even if, as a haunt owner, you can't pay, you can incentivize it.

Learn from Theater Directors

It all revolves around making connections, getting exposure within your community, and keeping you visible in the non-haunt season. It also gives you the opportunity to work with other directors. I often hear haunt owners say, "The people look right, but I can't get them to do what I want them to do." Well, that's what a director in local theater does—they get actors to do what they want them to do. If you're a haunt owner and you want to learn tricks of the trade, work with other directors. Even if you don't have the time to commit to doing the show itself, some theater companies or directors might just let you sit in on a rehearsal, and you can kind of peek over their shoulder. Again, a director's job is the same as a haunt owner's or a casting director's job for a haunt—to make the actors do what you want them to do, do it consistently, do it well, but not go too far.

Don't Be Afraid to Share

The other thing that's important to recognize about the overlap of theaters and haunts is there are a bunch of shared resources—things that might save you money or save the theater company money. Don't be afraid to share. Let me say that again. Don't be afraid to share. Many theater companies have costume departments and costume storage in which they have costumes from their old shows sitting in plastic tubs or, if they're lucky, hanging on racks. Either way, they're in some warehouse somewhere gathering dust. If you, as a haunt, have some stuff and they have some stuff, maybe you can work out a way to share costumes.

Often theater companies decide to get rid of their costumes in storage. This is also true of theme parks, especially small theme parks. That's a perfect way to get costumes. I just recently got a ton of really cool costumes absolutely free from a local cruise line. They were clearing out their costume warehouse, and they called several local theater companies as well as me and offered these to us. The great thing is, when theater companies, cruise lines, theme parks, or whatever are getting rid of their costumes, they're already distressed, so all you have to do is dust them down a little bit more, throw them on your actors, and you're good to go.

Theaters may also be looking for specific props you might have as a haunter, but they don't. Every now and then they might need a skull or a vintage Ouija board or a crucifix. These are the kinds of things that haunters may have as props in their haunt if they keep their haunt up year-round or in storage if they don't that could be loaned out to the local theater company.

So, create that sharing environment with costumes, props, scenery, lighting, whatever. Again, you can create win-win scenarios. As I've said many times, sharing doesn't diminish what you have. Sharing increases what you and other people have.

Haunts and Theaters Source Much of the Same Stuff

Another thing to be aware of about theater companies is they're sourcing a lot of the same stuff that you are. They need makeup, you need makeup; they need costumes, you need costumes; they need paint, glue, nails, and whatever, and they may have sources that you haven't found yet. They may have opportunities or vendors you haven't discovered yet and vice versa. For example, their lighting designer may want some sort of tiny lighting fixture instead of the giant stage fixtures that are usually available in theaters, and they don't know about Gantom's little LED color-piano fixture. You, as a haunter, can share that resource with them. They may have really good makeup sources, whether locally in your community or ordering directly from the manufacturer. Depending on how involved you are with them, you might be able to work together to do some sort of group buy and can get a better price. You *both* save money.

Many theater companies have audio that's set up in their theater, but they rarely have the tiny speakers they might need for what I call practical audio—things like a phone ringing or a gramophone. That's something many haunters may be able to share with them—those tiny, rinky-dink, computer speakers we've all used for something at one time or another. You can lend those to your theater company and maybe borrow their great Dracula cape during the haunt season.

Sponsor One Another

Another way the theater and haunt community can share is to sponsor one another. If you're involved with a for-profit haunt, and your local theater company is doing Dracula, Hunchback, or whatever, why not buy an ad in their program? That's kind of a no-brainer. Later, see if they want to do a sponsorship for your haunt. You may find that people want to do a tit-for-tat sponsorship. Obviously, you don't want to advertise in a children's theater program unless you have a family-friendly haunt. If your haunt is blood-soaked, you really don't want to be advertising it in a production of Hansel and Gretel. It does have a witch, I'll grant you that, and it does have the eating of children—hmm, maybe that's not such a bad idea. Joint sponsorship is a great way to raise the profile of both the theater company and the haunt. When it comes to things like printing, theater companies may have ways to get things printed cheaper if they do them in bulk.

Do a Cool Fundraiser Together

As you can tell, I think there's a lot of missed opportunity here between theaters and haunts, because there's an overlap of those audiences. As one more example, I offer this: Theaters are always trying to raise money, and haunts are always trying to raise money, so why not work together to do some sort of really cool fundraiser during both of your off seasons? All it requires is the space, some actors, and a little bit of rehearsal. Theaters, when they're not producing shows, are open spaces. Most haunts are always looking for spaces to set up. One cool thing to do in theater spaces is staged seances. You could put a table on the stage, make it a high-end fundraiser, and invite the board members. Or, wouldn't it be cool to have a haunted attraction and a theater come together to do a night of Edgar Allan Poe? Get some of your great queue-line actors or some of the actors from the theater company to work together and present readings of The Raven or The Tell-Tale Heart or whatever, and split the revenue. It would cost very little to do. Please, please, please, let me know if you do this, because I'd love to come out and read The Raven. I don't care where you are, I'd love to come do it.

Chapter 2

A Haunt Might Be Seasonal, but Haunting Is Year-Round Work

Even though most haunts are only open during the Halloween season, we have to work on them year-round. Around the beginning of each year, we start to think about what we can do as haunters to get ready for what's coming up. We're all just twitching and itching to get back into haunt season, right? In this chapter, I'm going to talk about shopping throughout the year for your haunted attraction and getting started on building your haunt well ahead of Halloween.

Start the Year by Planning for Your Halloween Haunt

Let's face it, there are things we all need and can only get at certain times of the year, and they're ungodly expensive. So, why not plan ahead and shop throughout the course of the year to take advantage of the after-season sales or whatever? To shop year-round, there are a couple of things you have to think about early on. First off, what theme are you going to embrace for the coming year? What's the story you're going to tell when Halloween time rolls around? You may be thinking, "It's too early to even think about that!" But it's really not, because, if you can plan ahead, you can find all kinds of cool stuff and save money. So, let's talk strategy.

Figure Out Your Story and Your Storage

To shop for your haunt throughout the year, you need two basic things:

1) A concept of what you're looking for, so you don't waste your money buying stuff for a project that doesn't happen (this is the voice of experience talking); and
2) a place to store this stuff and some storage tubs that stack neatly so your spouse doesn't yell at you for buying all this crap and leaving it in the living room year-round.

So, you first need to figure out what your themes are, what your designs are, and what you're going to need. That way, you can shop in a timely and cost-effective manner. Then there's the storage issue. Depending on where you live, you might need climate-controlled storage, because otherwise things mold. The werewolf mask will be furry—not with fake fur but with some kind of green fuzzy stuff that grew there. I strongly recommend that, the moment you get something, put it into a plastic storage tub. Cardboard isn't good, because critters can chew through it. Just after every major holiday is a great time to get those big plastic tubs with lids at Walmart or Target or wherever. I like the ones that have lids with handles that flip down to hold them shut. This makes them easier to stack, and you can label them, so you know what's in each one. With transparent plastic tubs, you can actually see what's in there, and you can label them, too.

Shopping for Your Haunted Attraction Year-Round

Now comes the shopping part, and I'm going to go holiday by holiday, starting with Christmas.

Christmas

Just before or just after Christmas is a great time to start buying stuff, because so much goes on sale—like up to 50% off—and there are some things you can only get at Christmastime. This isn't just for the cheapskates who want to save money; this is also for the practical people who are looking for things they probably won't be able to find the rest of the year.

The first thing I think of is lighting. At Christmastime, you can get all kinds of relatively inexpensive, somewhat disposable—if you need it to be—lighting that can work really, really well in your haunt.

You're probably thinking, "I don't want Christmas lights in my haunt." But, you might. Here's the thing. If you take a string of Christmas lights and bundle them behind a piece of scenery, you have a great source of indirect lighting. If you have the opportunity to get twinkling lights, you can use them to create a fire effect by putting them in a tiny enclosure or behind something. If you put Christmas lights behind scenery or build scenery that will hold them properly—rather than hanging them in strings, which I hate—you're in great shape. You can even use Christmas lights with a control panel if you're doing something with a sci-fi theme. You can use those little rice lights—the tiny, individual units that are strung together with copper wire. Quite often, they're battery powered. These are amazing if you want to do things like jars of fireflies or anything ethereal or ghost-like. These are amazingly handy, and they're really hard to find at a decent price except at Christmas.

Projector Lights

The other thing that's really cool are those projector lights you see at Christmas that have cartoon graphics of snowflakes, pumpkins, Santa, or whatever. I'm not a huge fan of those, but they can be useful. I like the ones that break up light and make it look like it's reflecting off of something else. These can come in really handy if you want to do a swamp scene and project the look of moving water on your walls. If you can get them at 50% or 90% off, do it. They usually come with yard stakes, but you can certainly modify those and use them indoors. If you have an outdoor haunt, obviously, that's perfect. You can just stick them in the ground and plug them in. They're LED, they run at very low power, they're easy to install, easy to circuit, easy to focus, and they have a surprising throw distance. Normally, they've got a sort of globe over the front, so they throw very wide, and they're good for creating an atmosphere. There are also multi-colored and laser versions that do that weird sort of green-and-red laser thing—which, by the way, looks really cool in a smoked room. If you've got the red and green, you can put them in a 3D house. They don't really read as 3D, but the lenses on Chromadepth glasses mess with them a little bit, so it makes them even more disorienting.

If I were going to do a haunt and I needed a new room, I'd go out and buy three or four of those laser lights right now, put them in a room, fill it with fog, and have them all going at the same time. It's a cheap, easy effect. What you get are these little pins of light shooting through the room and moving, and, if you put them at different angles, it's amazingly effective.

Battery-powered Lighting

Continuing on the lighting subject, I always want to know what I can get that's battery powered. I don't like to necessarily think of lighting just for lighting purposes; it's also cool for costume purposes. You can illuminate a mask or a costume with battery-powered lighting. This is extremely effective for strolling characters. I like to self-illuminate strolling characters, because you don't have to worry whether they can be seen. You don't want to wrap them in Christmas lights, but you can put the lights behind a translucent fabric or in the eyes of a mask. There are these mylar masks that are just a blank face. If you put lights behind those, it's a pretty cool effect. You can only do this with battery-powered Christmas lights, and the only time to get battery-powered LED Christmas lights is immediately before or after Christmas.

LED candles and good flicker candles are super cheap around Christmas. Battery-powered, LED flicker candles are very useful, especially if they have a remote control. You can turn them on or off, you can set them on a timer, and they're often dirt cheap. I realize it's much better to wire them into your board, but, if you're operating on a budget or, at the last minute, you realize, "Oh crap, this room is too dark. Let's put in some candlelight," they're great to have in your back pocket. I like the ones that are made of real wax, because the LED is sunk down into them, and it makes it look far more realistic. You get that flickering, candle-like light through the real wax candle. You can get these year-round, but they're harder to find and more expensive, so it's best to buy them at Christmas.

Tricks with Fake Trees

Another tool I absolutely love—especially when trying to create the illusion of the outdoors indoors or in a completely dark room that people have to feel their way through—is artificial Christmas trees. They're an amazingly cheap way to create texture. You can put them along a back wall and shine light through them to create the vibe of being out in the woods. You can line walls with them so guests can feel their way through, and they're sort of prickly and weird. Don't buy them new at stores. Go to the Salvation Army or a resale shop. People are getting rid of artificial Christmas trees all the time. You don't even need to spray paint them black if you don't want to. There are all kinds of ways to use artificial Christmas trees.

Remote-controlled Outlets

Remote-controlled outlets work really well in haunts and escape rooms. Everybody wants to switch on the Christmas lights without having to go around the house and plug this in, flip this switch, turn on that breaker, and blah, blah, blah. If you've never used or seen these, they basically plug into an electrical outlet, and you plug whatever it is you're trying to trigger into that. They don't have to have a line of sight, so you can keep the remote in your pocket.

Now that more and more is LED, remote-controlled outlets are popular. These are expensive at any time of the year, but they're the most cost-effective after Christmas. Get them while they're on sale, because they're incredibly useful—especially in an escape room with an actor in it. You don't need to have triggers for things. You plug them into this outlet, the actor has the key fob in their pocket, and they just hit the "on" button whenever you want that trigger to activate. This releases or turns on a mag lock and plays a recording or whatever. There are a million and one things you can do with remote-controlled outlets.

Spray Snow

Spray snow is getting harder and harder to find because it's probably carcinogenic or toxic in some way. However, putting that spray snow on windows to make them look frosty works really, really well when you want to create a silhouette behind a piece of glass, plastic, or plexi. Get a couple cans of spray snow while you're shopping, because it's kinda neat.

An Aside: Thoughts on Christmas Haunts

I don't care for holiday-themed haunts, because they seem like a gimmick unless there's a really good story that takes you on a journey through various holidays—or even takes you to Christmas in October. However, if you want to do that, Christmas is the time to pick up your Santa suits, your Santa beards, your elf costumes, and all that sort of crap, so you don't have to build them. You just have to distress them and make them look like Santa threw up in his own beard. Which, if I were to do a Christmas haunt, is probably what I'd do. I'd do homeless Santas, an army of homeless Santas. OK, maybe I've changed my mind. Maybe I want to do a holiday haunt. If there's anyone out there who wants to hire me to do a holiday haunt, please contact me. I'll be happy to write that and install that for you, because that would be cool—an army of homeless Santas that rob and kill people. I'm kidding. I'm not going to do that.

Valentine's Day

You may be asking, "What on earth can I get for my haunt that has to do with Valentine's Day?" Well, one thing you can't get any other time of the year is heart-shaped candy boxes. Now, I have a quirky, dark sense of humor, and I think heart-shaped candy boxes with real bleeding hearts inside of them is pretty cool. Not real hearts. I'm not saying let's load them up with human remains. I'm saying, let's load them with things that *look* like human remains. If you have any sort of love story in your haunted attraction, this could be a prop. So, grab them up on February 15th, because they'll be like 90% off. Eat the candy and save the box.

I strongly recommend you get a traditional kind of box—not an Avenger's heart-shaped box—unless that fits in with your storyline or theme. If you have a standard heart-shaped box, you can always use it if there's a love story going on. It's kind of a fun little wink to the blood and guts. You can fill it with severed fingers or whatever. You can gross them up pretty easily. Heart-shaped boxes can serve as a prop or set dressing in many, many different themes.

Artificial flowers are sometimes less expensive around Valentine's Day, although you can get them at other times of the year. Using artificial flowers in haunts is really effective, because it throws people off. It's like, here's something we think of as pretty, and yet it's tied to something we think of as decaying and disgusting.

Since we're talking about Valentine's Day, that brings up the topic of "personal massagers." We're all grownups here, so we can talk about this. Personal massagers are great to use in haunts. You can put one into a costume and, when the character touches you, you feel that brrrrrrrrrrt. You can also use them as super cheap animations if you can find the ones that move in a swirling and twirling manner. You can use those to make really inexpensive animations you can turn on and off.

Continuing on this theme, we all know the best way to protect a prop is to cover it with KY jelly, the water-based, personal lubricant, because a) it doesn't hurt most props, because it's water-based, b) when guests touch it, they immediately go, "Eew!" and they don't touch it again, c) it washes off, and d) it makes things look snot-covered, and that's always cool. So, if there happens to be a Valentine's Day sale on personal lubricants, that's a great way to protect your props and add a snot layer over pretty much anything in your haunt.

St. Patrick's Day

In March, there's St. Patrick's Day. Again, you're probably thinking, "What in the hell is there about St. Patrick's Day that I can include in my haunt?" I'm from Chicago, so the first thing I think of is green beer and dyeing the Chicago River green, which, interestingly enough, uses a chemical that starts off as orange. The only reason I put St. Patrick's Day in here is because you can occasionally get some leprechaun stuff that's kind of fun. If you've got a leprechaun theme going—or you think you might—and you want a little evil troll or something like that, you can include the ears and noses and that sort of thing. Plan ahead, because this stuff is hard to find except around St. Patrick's Day.

Easter

Many of you know I have a strong affinity for rabbits, for several reasons. I was born in the year of the rabbit, and I was a magician for many years. As part of my act, I had a rabbit that was probably one of the meanest creatures on the planet. I still have scars on my arm from where that little stinker scratched me with his claws. I was also the puppeteer for Bunny Rabbit in the all-new Captain Kangaroo, which was on Fox Family Channel for a while and is an award-winning children's television program. My right hand received an award, and I was very proud.

Of course, Easter is a great time to get rabbits (not real ones, of course), and I'm always looking for ways to incorporate rabbits. Pretty much every haunt I've done over the last few years has a rabbit in it somewhere, and I like to think of it as my signature. After Easter, I always go looking for rabbits—usually stuffed rabbits, because I think children's toys can always be creepy. There are some really creepy stuffed rabbit toys out there, like the ones with plastic faces that almost look human and are stitched to fabric. Those are hideous.

Anyway, go out there and get your rabbits. You can get realistic ones that you can disembowel and fill with guts. That might even work if you don't get realistic ones. Get one that looks like a cute child's toy, rip it in half, fill it with Great Stuff or Silicone, put a little personal lubricant on there so it looks wet and gooey, and then place it next to a child's bed. Now, *that's* fun!

Don't forget Easter eggs. You're probably thinking there's nothing scary about plastic Easter eggs. Wrong. If you make your own masks or props, and they involve creating monsters, the cheapest and one of the most effective ways to make large, bulbous eyes is to use half a plastic Easter egg. They come in many colors as well as glow-in-the-dark. You can get them in mylar-covered silver if you're making an alien or a robot. There are eggs that don't just open around the width but along the length, so the two halves are almost almond-shaped. Those make great eyes, and you can build lids over them with latex or silicone or whatever. So, get those plastic Easter eggs, because, when you need them, it won't be Easter.

They are also giant, inflatable eggs that you can get at the dollar store around Easter. Those make great alien heads, or you can use them as a start for a mask. I've seen people use those as a form to make a papier-maché animal skull. They'll use the round part of the egg to create the top part of the skull and build on that. It gives you a nice form, and it's dirt cheap.

Fourth of July

There's nothing much happening in May or June, so that brings us to July 4th. The only thing I could think of around the July 4th holiday that might be helpful to a haunter—other than fireworks, if you want to go there, which I don't recommend because of safety issues—is bunting. Bunting is those red, white, and blue banners that are draped on grandstands or porches. That's really cool if you happen to have a scene where you have an official who's making an announcement about how bad the zombie apocalypse is or something like that. Bunting works really well for scenic decor, and you can't get it, affordably, any other time than the 4th of July.

Summer—The Time to Prepare for the Halloween Season

Summer is when we should be actively preparing for the upcoming haunting season. By this time, all of the major theme parks and scream parks have completed their auditions, and they're starting to release information about this year's haunt season. By the end of summer, you should have all your changes and designs complete for the season ahead with an eye toward the implementation stage. At Howl-O-Scream, we used to say that all of our top-line concepts had to be done by the end of January or beginning of February, and by the time summer events at the theme park started to slow down or had already closed, we could shift all of our labor and energy into the creation of the Halloween event. If you do Halloween and also a Christmas event, your changeover time is short.

The Importance of Auditions

I have an entire chapter later on in this book about auditions, so I'm just going to talk a little bit about this topic here. I'm a proponent of doing auditions for a number of reasons. Chief among them is I feel this is best way to find the best cast possible. I have all of my characters in each room planned out ahead of time, so I know what each of their traits are, what their costume is, and what their props are. It's important for me to find the right person for the right role. My thinking on this is explained in my recently published book, *Follow the Story*. I'm all about the story.

So, I make everybody audition, including my volunteer actors. This way, I make sure I have people who aren't only the right people from a performance standpoint but are committed enough to show up for an audition and stay through the season. Auditions are also an early way to help promote your event. You might even get some media attention. Often, the news story will go like this: "You're not thinking about Halloween, but the folks at Busch Gardens Howl-O-Scream are." That's a great way to plant seeds in July or August for your Halloween attraction.

In some states, high-school students receive volunteer hours for performing in a haunt. You can partner with a high school and get some of the drama students or the class clowns—those larger-than-life youngsters—and provide them a way to channel their energies *and* put in their volunteer hours.

My auditions consist of a series of improv games. I've been casting and training people for so long now that I can pretty much tell within the first three minutes of the audition whether someone is hirable or not. By the end of a 10-minute audition, I can usually tell what kind of role they're going to do best in.

The cast will make or break your haunt. This is something I feel very strongly about. As you may have heard me say before, if you give me three good actors and a candle, I can scare the crap out of you. Make certain your actors work together as a team and they've got each other's backs. Scare acting is a team sport, and there's no room for grandstanders, showboaters, or divas. The audition process makes sure everyone starts on an even level. Also, in my opinion, when people are chosen to be part of a cast, they feel special. That being said, plenty of haunters get great results without holding auditions.

Start Your Marketing Campaign

Once your casting is complete and your construction is underway, try to get ahead of the game with your marketing media. I like printed material for marketing. Some people do flyers and posters, but one of my favorites is party hats, which I think is absolutely brilliant. With high-school students, printed material like a hat will show up at their parties. Posters and fliers work well with older audiences.

Printed material can be especially effective when put up in record stores, comic-book stores, bars, or in a university area (on the university activities board). I've also heard that table tents can work well in the right restaurant or bar.

Printing can be done either locally or by an online vendor like Vista Print. [Full disclosure: I don't get any kickbacks for mentioning this company.] Local printers and online companies often have sales on print runs, so start paying attention to any discounts. Your bricks-and-mortar printer might be able to turn a job around faster than an online vendor if you need something in a hurry. Know your printing needs and deadlines, so if you see a sale offering 40% or more off the regular price, you can spring into action. When I had a booth at the Transworld show, I waited until Vista Print had a sale on retractable banners and got my banner for 50% off. Get on the email lists of printing companies, and watch for the sales.

Business cards are a great way to promote auditions. They can be left around at high schools at the beginning of the academic year.

Jump on the media layout on your computer and continue to craft and fine tune your message. Before things get wacko-gonzo crazy, put together five different ideas for whatever advertising you'll be doing: flyers, posters, banners, etc.

Share your first marketing message when you're still weeks away from opening. A second can be shared two weeks out. Then do another one for opening and another for what I call the hump—the middle of the season when your guest flow is starting to slow down. Do one more blast on the final weekend, which is your last chance. Get them done now, and plug them in at the appropriate times.

Your Best Marketing Resource

Ultimately, the best marketing resource is your cast, because they're the folks that are the most excited about your haunt. Some haunts do profit sharing. If that's the case with yours, your cast is going to want a gazillion people to come out and experience your haunt.

You can provide your cast members with images to post on social media. Allow and encourage your cast to post images of themselves with the haunt's logo. Give them some ownership, a brag tag that says, "Hey, it's me. Come see me, friends." A cast of 50 who contact five people, each of whom contact five more people, can soon make the message viral. It's a powerful driver for ticketing—online or otherwise.

Providing tee-shirts to cast members by September is another great marketing tool. Shirts can be ordered in bulk and serve as walking billboards. They can even be sold as merch. This is part of broadcasting a consistent message: "We're the best haunt in town."

Pins are a cost-effective way to get your logo out there. I have *A Scott in the Dark* candle-bulb pins with me at all times. I hand these out to as many people as possible, because it's a great way to build brand recognition.

Look for Partners and Sponsors

You can also think of reaching out to partners as part of your marketing strategy. Don't consider other haunts in your area solely as competition—the enemy—but as businesspeople in the same ecosystem as you. If you're both doing good work, it will only expand general interest in haunting. You can cooperate with these partners to grow the demand for more haunting in your area.

Try to recruit local vendors to help market your haunt. If you have a small-town haunt, perhaps you could have a local ice cream shop create a sundae filled with gummy worms and bats and skulls and name it after your haunt. The customer buying it might get a 10% discount to visit your haunt or something like that.

For more mature audiences, consider teaming up with a bar. See if a local tavern will name a drink after your haunt or allow you to put up posters and a display featuring one of your key characters. Your greatest strength in finding a sponsor is to tell them about last year's attendance. There are many ways to come up with a mutually beneficial arrangement.

Use any reason you can think of for you and others to talk up your haunt. When you put up your posters, fliers etc., document it on social media. Example: "Here we are putting up posters at Bob and Martha's record store." Or, if a bar agrees to name a drink after your haunt, take three cast members in full costume and makeup to the bar, have them test that drink, and videotape the experience. The more you talk about your haunt, the more other people will talk about your haunt.

The biggest haunts, scream parks, and theme parks have sponsorship deals with Coca Cola or Pepsi, but this is arranged regionally, believe it or not. SeaWorld in Texas has different corporate sponsors than Busch Gardens in Tampa or Busch Gardens in Williamsburg. Most distributors are willing to put bottle hangers, stickers, or wraps on their products. Strategies like, "Show up with an empty can of Coke and get 10% or $10 off" can work effectively.

Coke people want to sell Coke, and you want Coke to promote your haunt. So, it's a win-win scenario. Sponsorships could work for you, but this requires getting in early. Summer might be too late, but it never hurts to try. If at first you don't succeed, chances are they'll remember you next year.

The Build

Eventually, you get into the construction phase of the season. You'll likely be doing much of the construction yourself, but don't hesitate to outsource fabrication to someone in your area who can create staging and deliver it in pieces. This might be more efficient in terms of time and money. Offsite construction and storage (for the off-season) could be a reasonable part of your business plan.

If you outsource carpentry or fabrication, go over everything with a close eye to make sure it all fits together as a unit. Too often, we see flats that don't line up. Their seams are open, so they look like flats rather than brick walls, because the pattern of the bricks wasn't lined up properly.

One aspect of fine finishing is getting your staging to look old and scary. I love going in and aging stuff, getting my Hudson sprayer and filling it with a little bit of acrylic paint, a little bit of water, and some Coke or diet Coke. I prefer diet Coke because it doesn't draw as many flies. The carbonation in the diet Coke keeps the paint in liquid form longer, so it drips farther down the wall. You can just spray in the corners with your Hudson sprayer and then go back and do another layer of another color. The carbonation makes it drip all the way down, which creates some really cool aging. It's quick and easy, but you can't do this, of course, unless all the walls are up.

Document the Good, the Bad, and the Ugly

Document everything you're doing—even those things that don't work out. You might find a way to make use of this information later—perhaps as early as mid-season. This means documenting every aspect of your construction. Get out there, take videos, and put them up on YouTube. Document the casting process with photos, video, and quality audio. Don't worry, you'll be nowhere close to giving away even a fraction of the scares in your haunt. I'm not talking here about a point-of-view walkthrough. I'm just talking about putting images and video on your social media from when you first start preparing through the end of your event. People return to social media when there's new stuff to see. If I get a message that says XYZ page has something new, that's where I go.

Summer is the season, because we usually think of things too late. When the Spirit store has taken over the first floor of the closed Sears in your local mall, you know it's time to really start to kick things into high gear. I trust I've jogged your memory or given you some new ideas or things to think about. As I often say, I don't have all the right answers; I just have a whole bunch of really good questions. Use your creative mind to come up with the right answers that work for you.

Keep Your Eyes Open All Year Round for Bargains

So, now we're closing in on the haunt season. By summer, most of us are doing our auditions and have built three-quarters of what we think we're going to build—even though we're only at half. We think it's three-fourths, but we're constantly saying, "Let's add that, let's improve that, and let's put more of this in." However, you should still be keeping an eye out for stuff all the time. I'm a huge proponent of shopping at the Salvation Army or any of the various and sundry thrift stores. It's a great opportunity to donate to a charity, but it's also a place to get stuff that's already beat up, so you don't have to destroy it from a costuming or scenic-design standpoint.

Some of these thrift stores have mailing lists, and you can receive alerts about sales. I get text messages from my local thrift store when they're having special sales. I know when everything will be 50% off, and I'll just walk through and see if I can find an unusual prop or costume piece. You can usually get men's suits and even formal wear. You can buy a suit for $1.50, clean it, distress it a little bit more, and save hundreds if not thousands of dollars on your costuming budget.

A lot of people get rid of their wedding dresses at these kinds of places. You can use those as props. They're great to put on a manikin and stand in a corner. If you've got an attic with a dress form, you can put an old, grungy dress on it, cover it with cobwebs and dirt, and light it properly (put some of those Christmas lights that you got on sale inside the dress to give an eerie glow to it) to create your own really cool scenic pieces without having to spend a bunch of money. You can take the money you saved and go to the various trade shows to buy one or two signature pieces.

Finding the Unusual on Vacation

Also, when you go on vacation, keep your eyes open. If, for example, you have a concept that's supposed to take place at Area 51 and you happen to go near Area 51 on your vacation, look around. You can pick up things like banners, tee shirts, or whatever, so you have those extra bits and pieces to make your scenic area seem authentic. If you're doing something about Day of the Dead and you happen to be in Mexico, that's a goldmine. You'll spend way more in the U.S. for the same items.

Keep an eye out for any period props or clothing that fit with the theme of your haunt. Those little details really help create an immersive atmosphere and, you know me, I'm all about creating an immersive atmosphere. If you want to set something in a diner, start shopping for tee shirts that have a diner's name on it. That way, you don't have to create them yourself.

Always Have Your Camera with You

This leads straight into my next piece of advice: always have your camera with you. Take photos of anything and everything you think might be haunt-worthy. I can't tell you how many times I've gone back to my own photos, printed stuff up, framed it, or used it as a flyer. I'll take pictures of old handbills if I'm in a museum, and I took tons of pictures of the Queen Mary when I was there on the ghost tour. You can either use them as inspiration or, if there's something particularly creepy you happened to catch on film, you can use that as a prop or blow it up and use it as a poster. Use your Photoshop skills to add something to the natural background.

We're haunters and, when we go on vacation, we just don't go to Walt Disney World. We go to weird places. We go to those creepy old historic buildings or to those lighthouses that supposedly have ghosts living in them. Taking photos is probably the best thing to do year-round and, when you take those photos, organize them in a way that you can find them.

So, now you know how to think like a haunter year-round everywhere you go. Each holiday offers something you can use in your haunt, and you know that, by summer, you need to be in motion with auditions and getting started on the build.

My goal is to be sure everybody has the most stellar haunt possible. But, what if you're not quite stellar? That brings us to the uncomfortable topic of criticism, which we'll address in the next chapter.

Chapter 3

CRITICISM IS A GIFT

Now I'm going to talk about how to deal with feedback, both positive and negative, and competition within the haunt industry. Lots of people think we're all out to get each other, but that just doesn't make sense to me. There are ways to give and receive criticism that makes it a gift, and I'm going to try to explain how that works.

When we put a lot of effort into something like a haunted attraction, we become emotionally invested in it. Whenever anybody says something positive or negative about it, we take it very much to heart. So, let's begin with people saying good things about your haunt. We've all had successes out there. When people say, "You're wonderful," or, "You're the best this or the best that," that's wonderfully powerful for your marketing campaigns—your Facebook page, your billboards, your advertising. But don't get too locked into that, because there's going to be someone just around the next corner who's going to say, "You suck." We need to take compliments with a grain of salt. I like to think of compliments as a head nod during a conversation. If someone is nodding in agreement, it's like they're saying, "Keep going, yeah, that's good, keep doing that."

In my opinion, criticism is a gift. That may seem weird, because it stings when you've worked on something and somebody absolutely hates it, doesn't get it, or just thinks you're a complete loser. Believe me, there have been many, many people in my career who've said, "You don't know what the hell you're talking about." The nice thing is, there have also been quite a few people who've said, "Scott knows what he's talking about, so listen to him." Whether you agree with me or not, at least I have a point of view. If you don't agree with me, I think that's a good thing, because I'm a firm believer that, for something to be truly great, someone, somewhere, has to hate it. If everybody thinks you're at 100% capacity and everybody loves you, that means you've hit mediocrity square in the bullseye. It may make somewhat good business sense in that you feel safe. Nobody is ever going to say Walmart is the best department store in the world, but it's clearly safe. Everybody can shop there, feel comfortable, and feel like they're getting a good deal. But no one is going to say that Walmart is the best place in the whole world to shop for everything.

The haunt industry is all about scaring people, and that means we're an emotion-based market. There are people who are going to be scared by one thing you do and other people who aren't going to be scared by that same thing. Some people are afraid of the dark, some people are afraid of snakes, some people are afraid of clowns, some people are afraid of doctors, and some people are afraid of monsters and aliens. There's always going to be someone who says, "That's not scary," or, "It's not scary enough." There are a number of different things you can do with that criticism, and I'll go into more detail about that shortly.

Basically, any criticism is someone else's perception of what you've done. Whether you're a home haunter, an independent haunter, or a theme-park haunter, you've been working your butt off and spending way too many hours and investing way too much of your time in making your haunt good. Then somebody comes by and glibly throws some sort of jab at it and says they don't like it. Your first response will likely be to get angry, but, if you recognize that their opinion is a gift, it makes it much easier to deal with.

As with any gift, you should always accept the gift of criticism graciously and say thank you. You can say, "Thank you for sharing your opinion," and even, "I've never looked at it that way" or, "That wasn't my intention, but I appreciate you sharing your point of view." Then, as with any other gift, you can use it to make changes. Or, you could decide, "This gift really isn't for me." You can consider what was said and determine if it's true and has value for where you want to go with your haunt.

Three Steps for Processing Criticism

This leads me to something I learned when I was in college. I had a phenomenal acting teacher. His name is Jim Hasselhoff, and he was my teacher at the Goodman School in Chicago. One of the things that Jim taught us is how to take criticism. He said there are three basic steps to taking any form of criticism or critique, and I've continued to apply his approach to this very day.

The first step is to open yourself up like a dart board. Allow anybody or anything to throw whatever comments, negativity, or positivity at you. Be open to it, let it all come in, don't argue with it, don't fight it as it's coming in. Smile, nod, and accept it all. That's challenging at times, especially if you aren't 100% confident about what you did to begin with. That's usually when people respond negatively—they realize the critic might just be right, and that hurts even more. Recognize this is someone's opinion and that you'll have the opportunity later to address it accordingly.

The second step of the process is to review and enact. Pluck those little darts off and find out what each one of them is. Was one of the criticisms that your haunt was too short? You can look at that and say, "I've got a limited amount of space." You might want to then consider if you're using the space to its fullest advantage. Then, look at this in conjunction with other critiques. For example, three other people might have said your haunt was too long. If so, that means it's probably about right, and those conflicting critiques cancel each other out. If you can get more information about these criticisms, that's even better.

The third step is to look at where the criticism or comment is coming from. If the commenter is used to visiting theme-park haunts, it's natural they might think yours is too short. Once you review all the comments—all the little darts that have landed on your own personal dartboard—you can figure out which ones are good ideas that you can actually enact. If someone says, "You don't have enough virtual reality in your haunt," that could likely be because of cost or what you're trying to do. Personally, I haven't found a virtual-reality experience that works for me. I haven't seen them all, so there's probably one out there that I'd find truly amazing, but it's just not what I want to pursue in my haunt experience or my escape-room experience or anything else like that. I think virtual reality takes us back into the computer, which is where atmospheric theater started in the first place.

Assess Which Criticism Is Valid and Which Isn't

I'm 6'4", so, if somebody at an acting audition says I'm too tall, there's nothing I can do about that, and it's not a criticism I should consider. When you're reviewing comments and deciding what you can enact, look at the content of the criticism not the way it's packaged. If someone says, "You're dumb as hell because you had only one zombie in your zombie room instead of 15," leave out the "you're dumb as hell" part and look at the content. Could you have had more zombies in that room, or was there a way you could make it look like you had more zombies in that room? Ignore the insults and look at the content. The same is true with positive criticism. If you've got people blowing smoke, that's great for a fog machine. If your guests or friends say, "It was really wonderful," ask them to be specific about what they liked about it.

Review and enact those things that make sense and you're able to do. After you've done that, forget all the critiques. Let them go. If you stay so focused on what guests say rather than on what you want to do, your storyline is going to get disjointed, watered down, or messed up. There's an old adage that says a camel is a horse put together by a committee. That applies here. Your haunt will become a camel instead of a horse if you pay too much attention to input. All you're doing is being reactionary to that input. You need to listen to it and enact it up to a certain point, but, if your entire creative design and structure is based on one comment after another after another, you really have no vision of your own. So, use the criticism as a tool—as a means, not as an end.

Listen to Guests as They Exit Your Haunt

When I was working at Howl-O-Scream, we had a simple way of dealing with guest comments. I spent a lot of time out in the park looming over guests' shoulders and eavesdropping on their conversations. That sounds creepier than it actually was. What I mean is, I spent a lot of time standing at the exit of a haunted house and listening to what the guests were talking about as they left. That's what you want to pay attention to. If you hear several people say, "It was a great house, except that last scare was lame," chances are good there's an opportunity for improvement there. Listening to guests at the haunt talking to each other is more impactful than what they post online or say in a survey.

Our model at Howl-O-Scream was based on three things: start, stop, continue. Start doing things that you're not doing that you should be doing, stop doing things you're doing and shouldn't be, and continue doing things that are working and build off them. Make it a, "Yes, and," scenario: "Yes, that works, and, if we do this, it will impact even more people."

Survey Your Guests, and Respond to Criticism

If you don't have an exit survey for your guests, you should do that. You have to have a thick skin to read these surveys, so you don't want somebody doing that who gets ticked off when a guest writes, "It was dumb. I wasn't scared enough." Surveys are important, because most haunt owners don't have the opportunity to stand around at the exit of a haunt—they're making sure the circuit breakers haven't thrown, all their actors are in place, etc. You can do a survey online with Survey Monkey, or you can do a written survey and have the guest either send it in, scan it, or leave it with you. Don't discourage people from sharing their opinion with you, because it's only going to make your haunt better if you use their input appropriately.

If somebody posts criticism in a public forum like Yelp, Facebook, other social media on your website or on somebody else's website, there are a couple of things you definitely need to do. First and foremost, it's okay to address their criticism. It's okay to say, "I'm really sorry you had that experience." Don't become argumentative. That serves absolutely no purpose. I'm saying this because I've made that mistake in the past. I was so close to the material, and I'd heard so many people tell me they loved it, that when one person said they hated it, the first thing out of my mouth was, "Everybody else likes it." That kind of statement only pushes that person farther away from you. They'll be less of a loyal patron. If you respond with, "I appreciate what you have to share. Thank you so much for sharing your opinion," that allows you to take a negative and turn it into a positive. It also might give them an opportunity to explain what they didn't like. Maybe they were angry because they had to park too far from your haunt, or maybe they were angry because it was really hot that night and they were wearing a jacket and it made them uncomfortable.

So, address online criticism, because it shows not only the person who gave you the critique but everybody else who's reading it that you, as a business owner, care. Everybody wants to feel as though they have part ownership. We have genuine fans in the haunt industry. Some people use the terms "fanboys" and "fangirls," and they make it sound almost like something negative. The truth of the matter is, it's not at all negative. It's very positive. I like to think of fanboys and fangirls as the next level of haunters. So, listen to your fanboys, listen to your fangirls, and show them you care. If they feel they have some input into what you're doing, they'll be far more likely to help promote your haunt.

Now, of course, when you address other people's critiques and comments, it helps you learn. For example, you could respond with, "I understand you feel the attraction was too short. What parts would you like to see expanded upon?" That input will help you make the experience better for everybody, and it turns a negative experience into a positive one.

I had a situation with one of my haunts in which a guest came up to me and basically read me the riot act. They knew who I was, they knew I was affiliated with this particular haunted attraction, and they said, "This was so lame. I'm an expert. I've done this, and I've been to that." I just sat there and listened to them until they were finished, and then I said, "I really appreciate you sharing your experience with me, because, obviously, you do know what you're talking about. You've been to a lot of similar kinds of experiences, and your feedback is valuable to me. Now, without sounding defensive, here's a couple of things you didn't see that, had you experienced them, might have changed your opinion." I then talked about a few things this person had clearly missed or not paid attention to. As we talked, they kept saying, "That's part of it? That's there? Oh, I missed that." I told them where it was, and they realized they were talking to their friend during that part. The more we talked, the more I was able, first of all, to understand what their perception was and where they were coming from, and they got a better understanding of how I put things together and how I felt about it. What's interesting is, even after giving me a really hard time, they went to their Facebook page, website, blog, and podcast and gave the event a very positive review. Now, they did mention that we'd talked, and they did mention there were certain things they found that were somehow lackluster or needed more attention, but they went on to say, "Make sure you keep your eyes open for this."

Guests Want to Know They've Been Heard

So, I basically took a situation in which someone who was trying to rake me over the coals, someone who wanted to challenge me and say, "I know more than you do"—which they probably did—and turned it into a situation where we became friends. Their thoughts were heard and incorporated. If someone has a gripe or a concern, the thing they want first and foremost is to be heard. They want to able to speak their piece and know that someone high up in the organization has actually heard it.

Here's a good example. When I was working in a theme park, one of the park presidents used to carry huge stacks of his own business card in his pocket whenever he went into the park. When a guest had an issue, he'd give them his business card, which had his cell phone number on it, and he'd say, "If you ever have another problem, call me and let me know what it is." I saw him do that, and somebody else who was with me saw him do that, and they said to him, "You're giving these front-line guests direct access to you as the president of a major theme park? Aren't you inundated with calls all the time?" He just shook his head and said, "No. I get a few, but, for the most part, if people feel they can call me with a problem, they don't. It's the people who don't feel there's anybody who wants to hear what they have to say that are far more of a challenge. By me giving them my business card, they feel like they're an insider and have a vested interest in the park, because they know me, the park president. And all it cost me is a business card." I thought that was really, really smart.

If you have guests who have legitimate concerns, hear them out. If you're face to face with them, take the time to listen. Nothing is more important—unless, of course, your haunt happens to be on fire. That's about the only thing I can think of that should take precedence. If those comments come across online or via email, take the time to address them, because it makes you look so much better.

What to Do When Other Attractions Post Negative Comments about Your Haunt

Another question many people have is, "What do I do if a competing haunt is posting negative things about my haunt?" To me, this is the saddest thing in the world. When one haunt creates some sort of false criticism of somebody else or false compliments about their own haunt, it undermines the real comments and the real compliments. This is a favorite maxim of mine: "What I say about my work always means so much less than what other people say about it." There were certain things I was proud of and really liked, and they flopped. There were other things that I was just so-so about, and people loved them.

If anybody is giving false commentary, positive or negative, it undermines the whole industry. If, for example, someone is making a negative comment about your haunt, and you discover the person who made it has never even been there and is just trying to tear you down to build their attraction up, the best thing to do is ignore it. Don't give it any more fire, because, for every action there's an equal and opposite reaction. However, if it's posted on social media or Yelp, you might respond with, "I'm sorry to hear this. What night did you attend? Please email me with further information." If you don't hear from them in about a week, you can post again with, "I still haven't heard from you. I'm hoping you'll contact me with more information." That's basically saying, "Ha ha! I caught you." That will usually stop any sort of what I call false negatives.

Although the haunt industry is hanging in there, it's in competition with so many other forms of entertainment. If we start fighting amongst ourselves, it just hurts us all. It makes us all seem petty. If you think you're doing good by tearing down someone else's haunted attraction to make your own look better, stop it. You're just making yourself look foolish.

Also, attacking somebody else's haunt can backfire. If you live in a town that has five or six haunts, and you go online and say, "This haunt is lame, stupid, overpriced, they don't have any scares," blah, blah, blah, the general consumer forgets which haunt you're talking about, so they don't go to any of them, including yours. What's good for any of us as individual haunters—whether it's a theme park or home haunt or whatever—is good for all of us. I've heard more than enough stories about towns that have lots of haunts within a certain radius. If somebody has a bad experience, they only go to one of those haunts, but if someone has a good experience, they go to multiples of them. You're only messing yourself up by trying to tear somebody else down. If you lack so much confidence in your own product that you have to tear somebody else's down to try to make yours look better, there's something wrong. You're clearly not working and focusing on making your product the best it can be.

It bothers me that this happens. When I was working at Howl-O-Scream, everybody thought we were at odds with Universal Orlando. That was simply not ever true. In fact, I have several stories about how their team and our team would meet up, work together, and have a grand old time. Every single year I worked for Howl-O-Scream, the Universal Orlando team—TJ, Michael Roddy, Mike Aiello, or Kim Grommel back in the day—would escort us around Halloween Horror Nights, and we'd do the same for them. We had the creme de la creme. It was hysterical, because there were times when we'd look at each other and go, "That's really cool. I've just been inspired by that." It would go back and forth. It wasn't, "Howl-O-Scream did something first, and then Universal stole it," or, "Universal did something first, and Howl-O-Scream stole it."

So, at one of those situations where we were escorting each other around the other's haunt, some members of the Fans of Florida Haunts saw us doing that and said, "I thought you guys were competing with each other." To a certain extent, yeah, we were, but, to a greater extent, if guests go to one of these huge, theme-park haunted experiences and don't have a good time, they won't go to the other. If they have fun at one, they'll go to both. It's that simple.

BE KIND TO YOUR COMPETITORS— IT ONLY BENEFITS YOU

Every haunter I've worked with has been so incredibly kind and open. They're always offering to give me a lights-on or behind-the-scenes tour, and I offer that to anybody and everybody I meet, too. If I have the opportunity or ability to share what I do with you to help you become a better haunter, that's great! Obviously, I can't give away all the proprietary secrets, but there really aren't a heck of a lot of proprietary secrets in this industry. If you think you're doing something that nobody else is doing, I'm 90% certain you're wrong. Someone else is probably doing it, and you haven't seen it yet. Now, that's not to say you stole it from anybody or anybody stole it from you. I'm not saying that at all. In fact, there was a year where two Florida theme-park haunted attractions had exactly the same theme for one of their houses in the same year. We were like, "How did this happen? How did they find out we were doing this?" The theme was Edgar Allan Poe and, come to find out, the Florida schools were focusing on Edgar Allan Poe that year. People's kids were studying the works of Poe and, lo-and-behold, that inspired both parks to do a haunt based on his works that same year. If you think somebody stole something from you, you're probably wrong. There's usually some other factor out there that made them think of whatever idea it is.

My point is, be kind to your competitors. Make it healthy competition, not unhealthy competition, because it's going to make you better, it's going to make them better, and it's going to make the industry better. I think the industry is recognizing this, and it's getting easier and easier for haunters to share their passion without feeling they're sharing any of their "proprietary" secrets.

Healthy Competition Helps the Industry and Helps Your Haunt

So, we've talked about critiques and criticism, real critiques and fake critiques, and false negatives. This all leads to the idea of competition. As I said, I don't believe competition is bad. I think it's good and healthy when it doesn't become a war. It keeps everyone on their toes. You can't rest on your laurels, because you know haunt X, right across the street, and haunt Y, which is about an hour away, are both going to keep ramping things up, doing new stuff, finding great new props and new training techniques for their actors, adding video, or whatever. This means we all have to keep raising our game. If there's good competition, it helps the industry as a whole, and it makes us a viable option instead of people going to a movie or bowling or whatever other leisure activity. It makes it so that coming to a haunted attraction, in a perfect world, is something people would do year-round.

Since we're out there "competing" with each other, why not work with other haunts to find win-win solutions? We must—and this isn't just in the haunt industry but the world in general—get away from the idea that for someone to win, someone else has to lose. That isn't true—or certainly not in business. Maybe it's true in checkers. If you create a scenario where your haunt and my haunt are both successful, that's great. Nobody loses.

People will argue with me—and it's a very valid point—and say, "There's only a finite amount of money people are going to spend on their leisure activities, and we're all competing for that same pool." To a certain extent, this is true, but I think there are greater competitors for that money outside the haunt industry. It's not just haunted attractions. Most people don't say, "I have X number of dollars to spend on haunted attractions." No, they have X number of dollars to spend on leisure-time activities, and we're competing with every other leisure-time activity—everything from putt-putt golf to go-karts.

So, back to creating win-win scenarios. For example, if you have the opportunity to co-opt your advertising, please take it. It will benefit you both. You'll pay half as much and get twice as much coverage. That's just the way it is. The people who don't want to do this are the people who are afraid their product isn't good enough. If you feel your product is as strong as your competitor's product, go to your competitor and say, "We have two very different style houses, but we're going after the same target market. How about we advertise together? You pay half, I'll pay half, and we get the same amount of advertising we had last year but spend half as much for it."

I just don't see how that can fail. People might argue, "What if I spend half on my advertising, and everybody goes to my competitor?" That will only happen if your competitor is better than you. Or, it means they're downtown and you're on a mountaintop with three parking spaces. If you're on a mountaintop with three parking spaces, you need to reevaluate your business model. You probably shouldn't be in the haunt industry unless you're doing something really, really personalized and special.

Collaborate with Other Haunts on Advertising and Tickets

Another option is a multi-house punch card. If you've got five haunted houses in your area, sell a punch card priced at the cost of only attending four of the haunts. The fifth one, in the mind of the guest, is free. What usually ends up happening is nobody goes to all five, and you pool the money amongst all of the haunts. If you want to have a third party or outside party hold the money and distribute it, that's fine. With a punch card, people who might never have come to your haunt get to experience it, because it gives them another punch in their punch card. It's also another way to co-opt your advertising. You're not just advertising your ticket, you're saying, "You can buy a ticket to only my haunt or get five haunts for the price of four." The other four haunts in your area are saying the exact same thing, so they're advertising for the other four as well as for themselves.

Some people don't believe this works. If you've tried it and evaluated why it didn't work, you have more knowledge than I do, and I'll sit down and shut up. The flip side is, if you haven't tried it or you haven't found the right playmates to make this work, give it a shot for a year. If it doesn't work in the first year, find out why. In my opinion, it's bound and destined to make things much, much better for you. I've talked to people who've made it work.

Go Enjoy Other People's Haunts, and Get Inspired

At the very least, visit the haunts you're "competing" with—not for corporate espionage purposes but just to enjoy them and see what works. Just as happened with the Universal team and Howl-O-Scream team, you'll be inspired by each other's work. Go, see it, and enjoy it. Let's face it, you wouldn't be a haunt owner if you weren't a haunt fan. You wouldn't be a haunt actor if you weren't a haunt fan. Go enjoy other people's haunts. If you believe only your haunt is worth paying attention to, my response is you don't know that if you haven't been anywhere else.

Whether it's a haunt or something else, the only way to truly eliminate an adversary is to make them an ally. There are times when that's not possible. I understand that. I'm not blind to the way things work in the world. If you believe someone is Satan incarnate, the only way to save them is to bring them back into the fold as an angel. Make sure you work really hard to eliminate adversarial situations, because they're such a drain on what you do, and it ends up hurting your ability to focus on what's important, which is the guests.

Be a part of making our industry better. As the industry gets better, you, as an individual member of that industry, will get better. When it comes to competition, criticism, and compliments, process them and use them as the gift they are, and move on. Don't make them your focus. Don't become retaliatory or argumentative. Criticism is the best form of research. It helps you make your product better. We want to be the best haunt in the world, and we want everyone to say it is. This is a lovely goal, but stay focused on the product. Don't stay focused on the criticism. Make sure you don't study only for the test but also study for the product, and focus on making the best product you can offer your guests.

Chapter 4

The Haunt Director's Role Is to Magnify, Not to Shine

We all think about haunt actors, designers, and people who build haunts. What we don't think about too often is what a haunt director does and whether we need one. As a haunt owner, this is something you should be considering. I think you need a director, and I'm going to explain why this often-unseen element is important for most haunted attractions and theater in general.

The Director Is the Lens, Not the Sun

Before we talk about direction for haunted attractions, we should start with what a director is and does. People have different views on what a director is and what their responsibilities are. What I'm going to share here isn't the be-all and end-all that leaves no room for anyone else's opinion. I'm going share my views about directors for haunted attractions or any theatrical experience—whether it's on stage, in a haunt, an immersive theater piece, or whatever—and you can see if it makes sense.

Here's what I think a director basically does for a theatrical experience: The director is the lens that focuses the light that everybody else brings to the project. I know that's kind of metaphorical, but think about it this way—the director is the person who takes all the sunshine out there and focuses it into a tight little beam that has the power to burn ants. Something like that. The director takes a bunch of random creativity and focuses it into something that's impactful and important.

A Good Director Makes Everyone Else's Work Look Better

All too often, I've run into directors in my career who don't believe their job is to focus the sun. They believe they *are* the sun, and the rest of the universe revolves around them. That's clearly not true. A good director is someone who's able to recognize their job is to make everyone else's work look better. Their job is to keep everybody on track. The director is the person who maintains and is responsible for the artistic integrity—and alters it, if necessary. Is the final product the same one that was talked about when you were all sitting around having drinks going, "Hey, let's do a haunt!"? Many haunts start that way—with alcohol—and that's probably why they continue that way—with alcohol.

The director is the one who takes the idea of, "Let's do a haunt about pirates who've passed on and are sailing in a ghost ship." I know. That's Pirates of the Caribbean. The director makes sure the haunt keeps to that vision and doesn't start introducing clowns, Freddy Krueger, and all that. So, first of all, the director keeps everything focused.

The Director Takes Responsibility for the Live Performers

Next, the director is the person who takes responsibility for the live performers. Directors work with all the other designers as well, keeping open and honest communication going with them, but the director is the one most responsible for the live performers. We'll talk about not just what the director does but how they do it in a little bit when we talk about actors. In my opinion, the director is the creative the-buck-stops-here kind of guy. In other words, if something goes awry creatively—for example, it hasn't been communicated to the lighting designer that there's a performer in a certain place, and the performer ends up standing in the dark—that's the director's responsibility. Yes, the lighting designer should read the script or venue flow to know what's going on, but it's the director's responsibility to make sure all the parts come together, stay focused, and create something amazing, terrifying, and true to the vision that was there from the beginning.

I've been very lucky, because, in most cases, I've directed pieces I wrote, so I didn't have to go back to the writer and say, "I want to change this, because this happened in rehearsal, or we discovered this." There are times where, in the past, directors would have to go back to the writer and say, "Is it okay if we change this or alter this?" It's up to you, but it's important to identify who has that final say—the writer or the director. Someone has to have the final say from a creative standpoint. Obviously, the people who sign the checks ultimately have the final say, but, as a director, it's your job also, especially if you're working in more of a corporate setting. I realize some of you are home haunters, so maybe all you have to do is go to your husband or wife and say, "I'd like to change this. Can I have another $75 to go to the hardware store?" You probably don't have to worry that much about this sort of thing. But, if you're in a corporate setting or you have multiple owners of a haunt, the director is the one who has to go to them and say, "We thought we were going to do this, but, when we put it into practice, we were having problems making it work, so here are some other alternatives."

Casting—Putting the Right People in the Right Jobs

I have a broad definition of what a director's responsibilities are. Some people just want directors to hire and train actors. I think that's a little short-sighted, because, all too often, the actors are doing one thing and the scenic, lighting, and audio are doing something else. In many cases, the actors are told to wear whatever they want in terms of costume. If you don't have a strong director, you don't have anyone to keep that in line. It's all focused on the overall story you're trying to tell. Yes, I realize that's the costume designer's job, but, if you don't have a costume designer and everybody is bringing in their own stuff, those decisions fall to the director. Again, in my opinion, the director is the one who's responsible for the creative success or failure of any haunted attraction or immersive piece of theater.

Let's talk about the practical side of what a director does. This is nebulous territory, and there's a lot of discussion about whether something is the director's job or the lighting or scenic designer's job or the actor's job. In my opinion, the most important job of a director is to put the right people in the right jobs—which basically translates to casting. I've done shows and seminars and talks on the importance of the audition and how to set up the actual audition process, and I'll talk about that in detail in a later chapter.

As the director, you have to continually find that balance between super-talented artists and really good people. If you cast people who are super-talented but absolute jerks to work with, they'll be a poison that spreads through your entire cast, and it will ruin your experience. No matter how good they are, if they're jerks, they're jerks, and they're going to ruin the haunt. On the flip side, if you're only hiring friends and people you really like to work with but aren't very good actors, that's going to lead you down a negative path as well.

In terms of casting, when a director looks at people who are auditioning, volunteering, or whatever, I think about 40% to 50% of what role the director puts them in is based on how they look. I know that doesn't sound fair. Whether we like it or not, 40% or 50% of casting is based on how the person looks.

When I'm casting, I also look for people's ability and willingness to follow direction. As part of the audition process, I usually try to change what I'm asking people to do and see how quickly they follow that change. I also like to do an interview where I actually sit down and talk to the person, so they understand exactly what the responsibilities are, what time

The Haunt Director's Role Is to Magnify, Not to Shine

they need to be there, that they have to learn to do their own makeup, that they have to do physical and vocal warmups so they don't hurt themselves, and the rules of the house—no touching or whatever. I explain all of that to them, and then I always ask if they have any questions or want to share information. You'd be surprised how many people will share information during the interview that you never thought to ask but that affects your decision to cast them or not.

Here's an example from a zillion years ago when I was performing in atmospheric theater in theme parks. I was at an audition, and the director—who was doing the casting—asked somebody next to me, "Why do you want to work here?" The person responded, "I was working in a water park, and the supervisor was a real jerk and treated me like crap. We didn't get along, he didn't like me, and I didn't like him, so I thought I'd come over here and work."

The director said, "You realize that the majority of performance here is for children. You're aware that you're auditioning for a children's theater experience in this theme park?"

"Yeah, yeah, I know. I don't really like kids, but I need the work."

Clearly, this is somebody you don't want to hire. If you're casting for a haunt and somebody says, "I don't really like working in the dark, and I don't like to be around people who don't drink," chances are good this person shouldn't be working in a haunted attraction. Just sayin'. So, when you're doing the casting, take a good look at the person, and make sure you're casting them in a role they can actually play.

I'll share with you one of my favorite dumb casting stories, and this was my own fault. I had to cast twins, and I found these two great actresses. They auditioned at different times with makeup that made them look alike. What I didn't take into consideration when I was casting was that one of them was probably four inches taller than the other. Not only were they to play twins, they were to play conjoined twins. Yeah, that was a really stupid mistake, but we were able to solve the problem by putting one of them in very high heels and the other in flats.

If you're casting a character that reappears over and over throughout the house and is played by different actors, make sure you stay within a height range and body type so, if you do casting over multiple days, you know they have to be between 5'8" and 5'10" and with an average body type—they can't be too large or too small. As the director, make sure you pay attention to the physicality of who it is you're casting and what they look like.

Casting is the first and most important job of a director—casting the right look, the right attitude, the right talent level, and how that all works in balance. Another thing I'd recommend with casting is, if you have a separate costumer, ask them to sit in and provide feedback. They might turn to you and say, "I'll never get a tuxedo jacket for that 7'1" person." That's just a very practical factor, so don't make a glaring error that's going to throw your budget out of whack or have people of extreme sizes—large or small—walking around naked because the costumer couldn't find anything for them to wear.

Working with Designers

The director should also work with the designers. In other words, once the collaborative idea has been set, the director works with the designers to make sure the lighting reinforces what the actors are doing, scenic provides enough hiding spaces for the actors, and the guest path isn't just a straight line. One of my biggest pet peeves when designing haunts is being sure the guest path winds so guests don't walk in and see a long stretch of nothing. As guests turn each corner, make sure they see something new. This probably comes from designing for a theme park for so many years, where we basically had to conga line the guests through. They had to be in a nonstop line, because batching was difficult with the capacity we had to accomplish. That's probably why I'm really big on twisty-turny pathways.

Work with your scenic designer so that your actors not only have a place to hide but also a place to escape. I'll tell you about another stupid thing I did. I wasn't the designer for this one; I was the director, but I just let it happen. We had an Egyptian-themed haunted house at Howl-O-

Scream, and I had a character that was a living hieroglyphic. (This story was written by somebody else.) The wall was carved out where the person would stand, and the actor barely fit into that opening. Obviously, going back to casting, the size of the actor was very important. What we hadn't taken into consideration was that when a guest got scared and threw their hands up to try to protect themselves, this performer had no place to escape to. That meant the actor ended up getting hit on a pretty regular basis, because they had no escape route. So, as the director, work with your designers to make sure your actors are taken care of.

If you use microphones, make sure you're working with your audio designer, so you have the information the actors need. Let them know how the microphone is worn and what they're supposed to touch as far as gain or what they're not supposed to touch. Most audio designers I know will lock the microphones so the actor can't turn themselves up or down. That's left to the powers that be, and the director makes adjustments as needed. If you, as the director, see something brilliant in the rehearsal process and you want to change something slightly or move a character to a different location, you should have the foresight and insight to do that and communicate it appropriately to everybody on the team.

Training Actors

Another important component of the director's job is training the actors. I'll discuss working with actors in detail in the "Operations 101" section of this book, but I'll say a few words here. If you have a stage manager or assistant director or lead or somebody who's in the house every night—and this person may be the director as well—involve them in the training. In large theme-park scenarios, where we have a multi-haunt experience with up to six different haunted houses and five different scare zones, each one of those has a stage manager. I train the stage managers first. I train them on what I expect each actor in each position to do. I make sure they understand perfectly, and then I let them train their own cast. I come through as the director by polishing and making suggestions. That way, everybody who's working—all of the actors—get used to going to one person with their problems and concerns, and I never have to hear, "Well, Scott said…"

That used to be a joke at Howl-O-Scream. Whenever actors wanted to do something the stage manager had told them not to do, they'd say, "Well, Scott said I could do this." It got to be so bad that there was a mantra that all the stage managers would use, which was, "Scott said, and Alex [Crowe] agreed." You eliminate all of that by training your stage managers and having them be the ones who train the actors. That way, there's no breakdown in communication or fabricated communication. So, get your stage managers involved with your actor training.

Give the Actor Ownership of their Character

Make sure you find the right balance between providing the actors with enough structure so they know how to be successful and yet leaving it open enough so their input can be incorporated as well. I know that may sound like a contradiction, but hear me out for just a second. For an actor to be successful, they need to have a certain amount of structure. Think of it this way: You're building them a jungle gym—or whatever that piece of park equipment is called these days—to play on, but what they do on that structure is up to them. The reason I say this is because my experience is that actors like to be right. If you say to them, "That's what I'm looking for," they immediately have a sense of success. Encourage them to take something in another direction, and reinforce what you like that they're bringing to the role or bringing to the character.

Ask Questions to Help Them Learn about Their Character

The reason reinforcement is so important is because these people are going to play these characters all night long, night after night after night— especially if it's immersive theater, like Vault of Souls. When we did Vault of Souls, these people played these characters for three to four hours at a time. There had to be enough connection between them and their character that they could believably play these roles for long periods of time. It also gives the actor a sense of ownership of the character. When I write characters, I'll say things like, "This is a voodoo queen. She's domineering and powerful and she uses spells." Then I'll insert a line that says, "Have the actor create three spells and have them tell you what those spells actually do." Again, give ownership to the actor to make it easier for them to play that character for long periods of time. I've put in enough structure to give them a sense of the character, but there's enough freedom for them to provide their input as well.

One of the most useful tools I've found for directing actors is using questions. Even if you have something specific in mind that you want, if you ask an actor a series of questions that lead them in that direction, not only will the actor feel they have more ownership, but they'll also discover and understand the nuances and subtleties you want them to have. In other words, you take them on a journey of discovery. During that questioning process, they often discover something even better than I had in mind. For example, let's say I want this character to be played as someone mentally stunted at the age of seven but who's hulking and threatening to the guests. I might start off by asking the actor, "How smart do you think this character is?"

"Well, he's smart enough to hurt people if he really wants to," might be the response.

"Okay, why, then, doesn't he have a gun or machete? Why is it just his bare hands, if he's that smart?"

"Maybe he's stronger than he is smart."

"Okay, so here he is, stronger than he is smart. I like that. That's the right direction to go. So, is he 80% strong and 20% smart? Is he 50-50?"

"He's probably 80% strong and 20% smart."

"If you were 20% as smart as you are now, that would mean you stopped being smart at what age?"

"Maybe seven or eight years old."

So, through a series of questions, I've led the actor to understand what the character is all about and given them a sense of ownership by going on that journey with me. It wasn't me just saying, "He's a giant baby." Now, sometimes you may have to do that, especially if you don't have a lot of rehearsal time, but I really do believe if you walk with the actor on the journey of discovery, you get a better product.

People might say, "I don't have time to do that with every single actor," and my response would be, "You don't have the time not to." Again, if you have any rehearsal process at all, by doing that, you lock in the character. You make it so both you and the actor understand who the character is and why that character is the way it is. Using questions is a very beneficial approach. You can also open it up so the actor can ask you questions. As an actor, I'll quite often ask the director something like, "Are you saying he's like a spoiled child?" I'll use analogies that help me put the character into words and relationships that my personal experience allows me to understand. Sometimes, as a director, I'm not clear about a character, but, during the course of my discussion with the actor, we come up with something better than I could have written sitting in my office.

Here's another important tip regarding directing actors: I try everything in the world not to demonstrate exactly what I want the actor to do. The only time I do that is if I'm dealing with actors who have no acting experience and will never get there on their own. In those cases, I'll demonstrate and let them pretend to do it after me. If you have anybody who has any experience at all and they're imitating what you do, chances are good they're not going to do it well. They'll have no sense of ownership, and I strongly recommend you don't have them imitate you if you can avoid it. Get them to where you want them to be by questioning them. This works so much better.

One more thing to focus on in training is to make sure each actor knows where they fit in with the overall story. What's the scare that happens before them? What's the scare that happens after them? Why is their scare unique? This way, that actor can prep the guests for the next scare, or they know what the guests are coming from so they can take advantage of that. For example, if you have an actor behind a drop door with a bright light behind them, and they know the room before them is really dark, the moment that drop door hits, they realize all the guests will see is light. They're going to have to reinforce that with some sort of sound or let the light come through and hit them first. They can stand up into the light, and it becomes a double scare. Making sure the actors know where they fit in the overall scheme of things makes them much stronger and sturdier. It will show those actors that you've brought them to a whole new level and given them the tools they need to succeed.

Also, I know it's not really the director's job, but it will win you big points with your cast if the director knows when and where the performers are on break. I'm a huge proponent of giving actors break time throughout the course of the night and having swings or double cast or whoever fill those holes, because that keeps everybody energetic throughout the evening. It's critical to know where the actors are on break. Are they standing next to the person who's performing for them? That's not really a break. Direct your actors to take their break in this trailer, this tent, this unused room, or whatever. Work with your scenic designers to make sure that's part and parcel of what's there.

Keep Actors from Going Rogue

Once the rehearsal process is over, the performance is locked in. In other words, don't allow your actors to randomly change things without any sort of outside eye looking at it. When they do that, one of two things happens: Someone gets hurt, or someone won't be in the right place at the right time. When I say someone gets hurt, it can be the actor or a guest, because the performer is doing something outside of what was approved. As a director—and, more importantly, as a haunt owner—this can be dangerous. If you don't know what your actors are doing, you're the one who will have to foot the bill for the lawsuit if something happens. So, make sure you give them structure, give them the freedom to develop, and, once it's developed, say to them, "This is where we are. If you want to change this, it must be approved before you do anything." If you've allowed them enough input, they've probably already made any changes they want to make.

After the haunt opens and you have guests, it's possible you may discover better ways for your actors to do something. As the director, you should be open to that, but again, once the haunt is open, the character is pretty much fixed in terms of how it's going to be played. There are five, six, 10, or 20 things they can do, so be sure your actors are clear they can't radically change anything without getting approval from the director, stage manager, or whatever your hierarchy happens to be.

The Magic of Positive Reinforcement

To keep people in line, I'm a huge proponent of what's called positive reinforcement. This is the way you train a dog, this is the way you train intelligent birds, this is the way you can train your husband or wife, this is the way you can train your kids, and this is the way you can train your actors. Catch them doing things right, and praise them for it. Reward positive behavior. If all you do as a director or a stage manager or any other person of authority is correct or punish people when they're wrong, all they learn how to do is avoid being punished. They may still do things wrong, they're just not going to get caught at it. If you reinforce positive behavior, they'll try to do the right thing, so they'll be rewarded. It's not about avoiding getting caught doing the wrong thing, it's getting caught doing the right thing. I always used to tell my stage managers, "Praise people publicly, redirect people privately."

Praise People Publicly, Redirect Them Privately

So, if somebody does a great job and gets a great scare, at your end-of-night meeting that day or beginning-of-night meeting the next day or when everyone is putting on their makeup, you can say, "I understand that Marsha over here got a great scare last night with that bunch of frat boys that came through. The big one fell to the ground and started crying—all because of Marsha. Good job, Marsha!" That way, everybody knows Marsha did a good job, Marsha feels good, and they'll go to her and say, "Hey, how did you get the big guy to fall down crying?"

On the flip side, say Marsha was busy texting in her hidey-hole when the frat boys went by, and I, as the director, was right behind them. Not only weren't they scared, they peeked around the corner and said, "Hey, she's on her phone. That's lame." After my head exploded, I'd pull Marsha aside and say, "You know what? Those guys didn't have a good time here. You missed an opportunity to scare them. Is that what you really want to do?" Do that privately, one on one. So, praise publicly, redirect privately. It helps with your cast's feeling of self-worth, and it also helps them work harder for you.

Maybe some of you are thinking, "I have volunteer actors, so I can't go that deep with them." Actually, you can. If you have volunteer actors, they're doing it because they love it. If you show you care as much about them as they care about the job they're doing, they'll do it better and will stick with you longer. Everybody likes positive reinforcement, especially if they're not getting paid.

Redirecting privately doesn't mean being a jerk. It doesn't mean taking the person into the back room and beating the crap out of them. And, by the way, when I say redirect privately, I don't mean walking into a crowded room and saying, "Excuse me, Joe, can I talk to you privately for a moment?" Everyone in that room is going to know exactly what that means: "Joe screwed up!" No, don't do that Mr. or Ms. Director.

Model the Behavior You Want to See

If, in your entire season, you have 10,000 people come through your haunt, that's 10,000 opportunities to do exactly the right thing and 10,000 possibilities that something will go wrong. The more consistent you are, the better your ratings will be. If everybody gets the same high-quality experience, nobody will get on social media and complain that your house is lame.

This is another of the director's responsibilities—you have to set the tone with your actors and staff. Part of setting the tone is doing what you say you're going to do. If you tell your cast to be on time, you need to be on time. Make sure your rehearsals start on time. Model the behavior you want others to follow. If you tell them they have to get along, take care of guests, and give 100% all the time, you, as the director, stage manager, or whatever, have to model that behavior. If you're sitting on your butt in the corner on your phone and telling your actors, "Get out there and give 110%. Hey, I just got an extra life in Candy Crush!" you're saying one thing and demonstrating something completely different. What you're demonstrating speaks far louder than what you're saying. Being the director doesn't mean you're less invested than the actors. You have to be more invested and focused on your job.

The sad thing is, being a director can be a pretty thankless job. The director is the first to get blamed when things don't go right and the last to get recognition when they do. If the actor isn't up to par, the director is the one who gets blamed. If an actor does a phenomenal job, they get the praise. I'm talking primarily about responses from guests. If a guest says, "The whole house sucks, and there was no focus," it's probably the director they're talking about, whereas, if a guest says, "Oh my gosh! Everyone scared me over and over again! What a great cast!" If you're the director, take that as a huge compliment. When someone says, "This cast works so well together," take that as a phenomenal compliment, too.

In closing, let me say this. If you're a small haunt, you may think you don't need a director, and you may be right. However, someone has to take on that role—whether it's the owner or the stage manager or, if you're a home-haunt mom, you become the director. Someone has to make sure the actors are working in cohesive synchronicity with everything else in the house.

Chapter 5

Choose Your Level of Extreme Early

Now that we have the larger philosophical points covered, it's time to shift into thinking about how extreme your haunt will be. How do you know when you've crossed over the line?

How to Determine What's Too Much

When it comes to the question of what's too much in a haunt, if you ask 15 different haunters, you'll probably get 14-1/2 different answers, and all of them may be valid. I have a strong opinion on this, which is—it depends on what's right for you, your audience, your demographic, your crowd, and what you want to accomplish. In the haunt industry, determining when something is too much is like asking somebody to identify the best kind of music. It depends on the scenario. If you're hosting a high tea in a really posh setting, heavy metal is probably not the music you want to have playing.

I've been to haunts where touching is allowed and haunts that are no-touch, and both types can be cool or not so cool. It depends on what you want to do, what you can get your cast to do, and what you think your audience wants. There's a lot of different things to consider. I've seen "extreme" haunts that seemed gimmicky rather than revolutionary. We're all looking for that next big soundbite to drive attendance and get tons and tons of people into our haunts, but it's dangerous to look for that in a gimmick.

Several years ago, they came out with the "free" haunted house—if it doesn't scare you, it's free. In my opinion, that's gimmicky. Nobody would argue that it's a great headline, and it draws attention. If anyone reading this made tons and tons of money doing this, please let me know I'm wrong.

Should You Allow Performers to Touch Guests?

Another issue that comes up regarding what's gimmicky and what's revolutionary is, "Should you allow performers to make physical contact with guests?" When I worked in theme parks, I was never able to design a house where guests could be touched, because there are all kinds of legal ramifications. Due to the number of people going through theme parks, there are concerns about safety—not just assuring guests are physically safe but that the park is safe from litigation. It makes total sense and, obviously, I think everybody wants to be free from litigation.

I've done haunts where performers can touch guests and haunts where they can't. If you decide your performers mustn't make physical contact, there are ways to get around that and still make guests feel as though they've had physical contact. One example is to use either air blowers or the AirZooka—that's the brand name—which is basically a plastic bucket that has a piece of tarp or Visqueen on it. When you pull that back and let it go, it shoots a blast of air. By the way, if you fill them with fog, they blow smoke rings, which is pretty cool. You can have a performer hiding in the shadows shooting that at people, and guests will swear they were touched when they weren't.

Another cool thing you can do if you choose not to touch guests is to use cat toys or feathers on long sticks to brush against a guest's ear. If you decide you don't want to run the risk of doing a full-contact house, these are ways to get around that but still interact physically with guests.

When you do full contact, one of the things you have to keep in mind is giving your actors and your guests parameters. In full-contact houses, it's basically lap-dance rules: the performers can touch guests, but guests can't touch them. You have to give your performers guidelines as to where and how they can touch guests. We want guests to feel frightened, but, in most cases, we don't want them to feel violated. So, it's an interesting bridge regarding how to handle that. When I did full-contact houses, I told the performers they could touch anything from the armpits up and from the knees down. This way, nobody is getting into a bad-touch scenario—"Don't touch me there. It makes me feel all tingly and inappropriate inside." I make a joke out of it, because there are guests who will complain about that even if it didn't happen. So, we made it clear to all the actors they may touch guests on the shoulders and arms but not on the torso area near any of the inappropriate parts, if that makes sense. We never had a whole lot of problem, because we made it clear to the guests before they entered the house that they'd be touched. They were told three times on site, and it was on the website and the printed material. Some guests actually got upset when they *weren't* touched, because they expected they would be. If there's a character who's, let's say, a dominatrix, and she doesn't smack you on the butt, you could get a little upset, because you feel you missed out on something.

You need to decide what's too much for you. What are you comfortable with as an artist and what are you comfortable with as a businessperson? Whether you do touching or not, there's a couple of things you have to keep in mind. First of all, it's dark in most haunts, so whether or not physical contact is made is harder to identify—was it physical contact with a person, or did the guest brush up against a manikin?

In no-physical-contact haunted experiences, I've discovered that the majority of times when guests believe they were touched, they were indeed touched by a person, but that person wasn't on the payroll. It was the person behind them in line, and because it was dark, they believed they'd been touched inappropriately. That happens quite a bit. Also, if there's alcohol involved on the guest's behalf, they may imagine they were touched or feel something inappropriate happened when it didn't.

Is touch revolutionary? Probably not so much anymore. Is it gimmicky? Probably not so much anymore. I think it's going to become more and more of the standard as long as we can keep the paranoid people under control—not only guests but also haunt owners.

Is It Revolutionary, or Is It Gimmicky?

In the days when I was at Howl-O-Scream, we did some revolutionary things like Alone and The Experiment. To my knowledge, Howl-O-Scream in Tampa was the first theme park to do a haunted attraction where guests went through by themselves. Is that revolutionary in the haunt industry? Absolutely not. Many independent haunts had been doing it for years. When you put it into a theme-park setting, it goes against the we-have-to-get-as many-people-through-as-possible mentality. When we did Alone, for example, we pitched it for about five years before it was actually approved. The park president finally said, "Yeah, go for it. Let's show them how scary we can be."

The Vault of Souls wasn't necessarily revolutionary, but it certainly was a different approach to haunting, because there were no jump scares or startle scares. For the first two years, it was all about the atmosphere, the elegance, and the paranormal side based on the history of not only the building but also downtown Tampa. It was an unusual experience, and that made it difficult at times to communicate to guests what they were in for. The ratings show that the majority of the guests thoroughly enjoyed that kind of experience. Our audience was targeted. The Vault of Souls didn't play well with teens who want the chainsaw and lots of gore. The Vault of Souls had none of that. We didn't call it "an evening of elegant fear" for nothing. It was targeted to a particular market.

Is It Storytelling, or Is It Just Shock for Shock's Sake?

There are haunts out there now where guests are tied up, waterboarded, or forced to eat gross things or drink a liquid from a feminine hygiene product. There are some houses out there that are really, really over the top. I think that's all shock for shock's sake, and I have yet to experience one or hear of one that embraces the concept of storytelling while doing that. To me, that's more fear factor than haunt. Now, there are some people who love and thrive on that. It's great for media if you can say, "We're the most disgusting, most vile, most over-the-top haunted attraction anywhere." And there's an audience for that. Is that too much, and do I condemn it? No, I absolutely do not condemn it, but I don't find it entertaining. I'm all for taking it to the edge, but don't take it past that point, because then you muddy the waters. Are you trying to scare people or just gross them out? Steven King once said, "If I can't scare you, I'll gross you out. I have no shame." I get that, and there have been plenty of times, in various and sundry haunts, in which I've used the gross-out factor.

In The Experiment, for example, at Howl-O-Scream, I had a room where one of the guests had to put their hand inside what looked like a garbage disposal to get the key to the next room. Then, of course, we flipped on the garbage disposal, and it vibrated. For me, there was something terrifying about putting your hand down that garbage disposal. Was it a real garbage disposal? Obviously not. Did we force anybody to feel pain? Absolutely not. In that same house, we had people dig through live insects to get the key to the next room. The Experiment was interesting, because it truly was an experiment. It was essentially a precursor to the adventure side of escape rooms. Escape rooms rely on two basic patterns—the puzzle room where you solve clues to move on or the adventure room where you have to do certain things to move on.

Eating pig's intestines, drinking curdled milk, being tied up and having my head held under water—I ain't gonna do it. That's not entertainment. To me, that's not even frightening. It's just annoying. I don't mean to bash anyone who's out there doing that, because some folks are being very successful at it. I say, "Rock on. You've clearly found your niche, so stick to it."

Understand Your Audience, and Have Appropriate Sensitivity

To me, what's more impactful or dangerous than the over-the-top, eat this or do that experiences are those that involve controversial topics. In the theme-park industry, we avoided violence against children and anything to do with religion, and we tried to keep violence against women at a minimum. We couldn't always do that because, some of our victims were played by female actors, but I tried to have as many male victims as female victims. No matter what you do, you'll eventually offend someone, and that's a difficult thing to deal with. We're not out there to offend anybody. We're out there to scare people. However, to scare people, we have to put them in scenarios that may be considered inappropriate or unpleasant.

A friend of mine tried to do a haunted attraction based on Nazi Germany, and it failed miserably, mainly because there's still a generation that remembers that very dark spot in our history. It wasn't scary. It was anger-inducing, because it was just too close to home. Was it terrifying? Absolutely. The atrocities that happened in that time and place were inexcusable and unfathomable. This was certainly not a form of haunt entertainment I'd recommend. I don't even know why they tried it, but they did.

Another good question is, "Should you include children in your haunt?" I always say, "A family that scares together stays together." I'm going to sound contradictory here, but, if you have a family with kids who want to go out and play just like mom and dad do—and they understand it's all pretend—I say, bring it on. That's super cool. The haunt industry is a great place for anybody who understands it's all just pretend. If your guests are parents who want to bring their kids, and you're able to follow the appropriate labor laws, go ahead and do it. I see no problem from a content standpoint.

It amazes me how often asylum haunts get letters from people who are involved with psychiatric care. If I do an asylum-style haunt, I set it in a different era, when the treatment of people with psychological illness wasn't nearly as humane. Even if I do that, someone will complain that it's disrespectful to people with mental illness. My response is that we're not going after people with mental illness. What we're doing is showing what happens when asylums go horribly, horribly wrong. Any of you who've taken a class from me or met me in person know this is my approach to creating any haunted attraction—pick a location, and add the phrase, "gone horribly, horribly wrong." If you do this, you can create a haunt out of anything. You're not presenting an asylum in a realistic setting. You're presenting an asylum in a fictionalized setting where things have gone wrong, and your message is, "This isn't right. This isn't how things should be run."

I've had people ask me, "Should I ever do a haunt about a current political situation?" I think you're going to run into huge problems if you do this, especially right now. We're very polarized as a country, so to do anything political is just foolish. It will either make people angry or make people laugh. I don't think either one of those is particularly helpful when you're trying to tell a scary story. We had a situation where we did a mortuary—which is one of the most common haunted-house themes—and some morticians signed a petition stating our attraction was offensive to their profession. A year later, another bunch of morticians contacted us and asked if they could create a publicity stunt for us. They said they'd love to come out and go through the mortuary—"Morticians in the Mortuary." So, it just depends on the individual and what ax they have to grind. The truth of the matter is, there will always be someone who gets offended or finds something to grouse about. The bigger you are, the more likely it is that people will go after you, because they think they can affect this behemoth of an event or get some money out of it—even if it's just getting their ticket price refunded. Usually, when you talk it through with those folks and explain the situation, they calm down and realize that whatever you're doing is all in fun or all in the name of theater—it's pretend.

How About an R-rated Haunt?

One thing I've never done but always wanted to do—or at least explore—is slightly more adult themes. I've been to one haunt that claimed to be R-rated. All they did was play R-rated films in their queue, and there were a couple of video splices in one or two of their scenes. If anybody reading this has done a scene that had, let's say, full-frontal nudity and only guests age 18 and up could go in, let me know. There are haunts in which guests go through naked on certain nights, just to make them feel completely vulnerable. That's an interesting gimmick, but I do think it's just that, a gimmick. I haven't had a chance to do that, but I probably would. People ask me, "Wouldn't you be even more scared to have the actors see you naked?" My response is, "If the actors see me naked, I'll be more scary to them than they'll ever be to me, I promise."

Although it's not necessarily a haunt, Sleep No More in New York City has scenes where both male and female actors are nude. There's a creepiness to the whole experience, but it's clearly not a haunted attraction. It's immersive theater. The first thing I realized when I walked out of there was how fast a group of people will get out of the way of a naked wet guy. He's just gotten out of the tub and is racing toward the audience that's gathered in his room. People parted like the Red Sea. Everybody was like, "Ahhh! I don't want the naked guy touching me!" The same was true for naked women, although people didn't move quite as quickly. I don't know if that's a social statement or not. Having nudity in an environmental theater piece is intriguing. It makes people feel more uncomfortable, but, at the same time, it titillates them and keeps them interested. I'm wondering how well that would work in a haunt.

I've done faux nudity and sexual situations, so, if anybody wants to do a haunt in the next couple of years that includes that, get in touch with me and we'll work something out. If you're able to do that with vampires, werewolves, or even zombies, it adds a level of reality that's really, really cool. I think it would be something fun to explore.

How Far to Go with Torture

There's always that question of how far to go with torture. If you've seen any of the Saw movies, it's obvious you can go pretty much anywhere you want to these days with torture. In my opinion, when we see too much torture, we become distanced from it. If you've seen Saw, *Hostile*, or any of the extreme torture flicks, you become numb to it after a while. So, I guess that means you can go pretty far with torture, because people look at it and say, "That's gross or that's cool or that's horrible. Next!" I don't think it makes a lasting impression on them.

How to Do Blood Effectively

People ask me, "How far do you go with blood? Should everything be blood-spattered and blood-smeared with intestines hanging off the walls?" There was a time, early in my career, where I would have said, "You should make it as bloody as humanly possible." Now that I'm a little older and the industry is more mature, I think blood should be used appropriately. Sometimes, less is more. If you have blood smeared all over the walls of a room, does the audience perceive that as blood or just red paint? If you have a scenario where you've got a manikin lying on the floor that's clearly fallen off a ladder, and there's a spatter of blood on the white linoleum floor coming from behind its head, that reads as blood not red paint. Let your blood be focused, so it tells a story. Guests should see it and immediate think, "I understand where that blood came from." If you do have someone covered in blood, it's more compelling to put them in a room that isn't. It's that juxtaposition of a pristinely clean room with someone who's literally dripping with blood because they've been eating the organs out of the dead body next to them or something like that.

If there's too much blood, it has an almost white-noise quality, in my opinion. If you want to throw in blood, guts, and gore, that's great, but make sure it's juxtaposed so people don't think, "Is that blood, or did they just paint the room red?" By the way, if you've got a room that's covered in blood, don't use red light, or the blood disappears.

The perfect example, for me, of how blood is effective has to do with the first time I saw John Carpenter's *The Thing*. It's an old film, and I saw it in a theater when it first came out. It was considered to be one of the goriest movies ever, and it was one of the first movies to get an R rating specifically because of the blood and violence—the blood, guts, and gore. You see scene upon scene upon scene of heads severing themselves from bodies, legs growing out of them, and the heads crawling across the floor. There's a dog whose face rips open and a creature comes charging out. To this day, the scene in that movie that just woogs me out is the one where they're trying to figure out who has molecules of the creature living in their systems, so they're taking blood samples. They take out a scalpel, slice off three people's fingers, and watch them bleed into a petri dish. Taking a scalpel and slicing someone's finger off makes me cringe more than watching someone's face explode. Why? Because I've never seen someone's face explode, but I've cut my finger, and I know how much that hurts. I know that moment of feeling the blade go through the flesh, and it makes me cringe. I cringed just now, thinking about it.

So, with extreme blood, make sure it fits within the context and fits within the story. Be as gross as you want, be as over the top as you want, but make sure it stays focused, so you don't work against yourself.

Limits in Escape Rooms

Many haunts are going into the realm of escape rooms and adventure rooms, and I think that's absolutely the right progression. One reason for doing this is it generates year-round revenue, which is smart, but I also think it's the next step in the progression of immersive or interactive theater. We're now giving people puzzles or challenges to explore. Which brings us to, can these go too far? It is too far to have a key hidden at the bottom of a water-filled toilet or a blood-filled bathtub, so guests have to put their hand in there and fish around for it?

We did this in The Experiment. We had a button that opened the door to the next room at the bottom of a really disgusting-looking toilet. You had to put your hand in the water and push the button. There were people who thought that was too over the top. For one thing, you have to have potable water in there and make sure it stays clean, so nobody gets sick. We set it up as a closed system with potable water and a real toilet that would flush after each guest. The water would go from one receptacle to another and, at the end of the night, we'd dump out the water in which guests had immersed their hands. We made it look as gross as possible, but it wasn't transmitting disease or disgusting germs in any way, shape, or form.

In escape rooms and adventure rooms, it's quite common for guests to have to dig through a cadaver to find the key or solve the puzzle for the next room. Again, we're going to have to start asking the same question— how far is too far? One of the earliest escape rooms was Escape from a Zombie. What's going to happen when it becomes Escape from a Zombie Who Can Touch You? Then it will be Escape from a Zombie Who Can Touch You and Is Covered in Ooze and you have to change your clothes while you're still trying to solve puzzles? With escape rooms and adventure rooms, we're going to go through the same growth process to keep finding what's new, what's over the top, and how far we can go.

Make Sure Whatever You Do Fits the Story

Whatever your story is, make certain that the level of over-the-topness fits it. For example, if you want to do a full-contact house where people are being grabbed and tied up, that has to make sense within your story. Be sure it's not just a gimmick to hold guests there while something disgusting happens around them. Going back to our asylum concept, put a guest in a straight-jacket and have them be the inmate. I had an idea years and years ago that I've never done—strap someone into a bed, have the bed on wheels, and push the bed through the haunt. Quite often in haunts, people want to run ahead to get away, but, if they're strapped into a bed, they'd be forced to move very, very slowly through terrifying scenes. If they were strapped in a bed, actors could get close to them without making physical contact and breaking that barrier of personal space. The guest wouldn't be able to throw a punch or injure the actor. All they could do is close their eyes and pray for it to be over. By the way, if anybody wants to do that bed thing, go ahead. Then call me so I can come out and see how it worked.

Once you're sure whatever it is fits your story and you figure out what you're comfortable with, train your actors to only go to that level and no farther. That way, if a guest complains or brings something to your attention, you can tell them how you trained your performers and find out if the actor went beyond that. If that's the case, you assure the guest you'll talk to that individual.

Market Your Haunt so Guests Know What to Expect

Once it all fits into your story and you've got your actors trained, the next step is to market your haunt appropriately. You've got to let guests know, up front, what you're doing and how you're doing it. You need to make clear if you have a full-contact, wrestle-guests-to-the-ground kind of haunt or it's an atmospheric, explore-on-your-own haunted experience with no touching. Make sure guests know, going into it, what to expect. If they don't, they'll either be disappointed or ticked off. This is probably the biggest challenge and most important message when it comes to extreme haunting of any kind. When you do your extreme haunt, market it appropriately, so you get the right audience for whatever it is you feel comfortable with.

I realize I haven't really answered the question, "How much is too much?" That's because there is no one answer. What's too much for me won't be what's too much for you, and that will be different than what's too much for somebody else. However, I hope I've given you some things to consider to help you decide how far you personally want to go in your haunt.

To sum up—no matter how extreme you go, make sure it's organic and not a gimmick, make sure it fits your story, and make sure you market it clearly.

Chapter 6

The Four Levels of Haunt—The Importance of Targeting One of the Four Demographic Audiences

Having determined how extreme your haunt is going to be, now it's time to decide who your core customer group is. Determining your core guest impacts everything at your haunt. In this chapter, I'm going to talk about the different levels and layers of haunts. Let's face it, there are all kinds of haunts out there for all kinds of audiences. I'm not talking about haunts that are more scary, less scary, more bloody, less bloody, too much, or too little. I'm going discuss the different audiences that a haunt can appeal to.

The Four Haunt Audiences

The way I see it, there are four, basic, haunt audiences—you can do a kids' Halloween event, you can do a Halloween event that targets tweens, you can do a Halloween event that targets what I call teens-plus (which is basically 18 to 35… or maybe 40, maybe 55, maybe 65, or, depending on how much you're into it, maybe 85 or 95), or you can do an adult, grown-up, Halloween event. What's important to be aware of is that each of those demographics views Halloween differently.

I was lucky enough to grow up in the era when Halloween meant trick-or-treating, going out and raising hell, and having a good time doing it. We didn't have to worry about questions like, "Is it safe for kids to be out after dark? Is there going to be a horrible drug in the candy? Will somebody kidnap us?" We'd go out, right after school, on Halloween, and our parents would give us our curfew time. Of course, I grew up in Chicago, so it was dark at four o'clock in October. We'd be out until whatever the curfew was, and that time changed as I got older. We'd be all over our neighborhood and adjoining neighborhoods getting as much candy as we possibly could.

I wasn't a toilet-paper-tossing hooligan. I wasn't that kind of kid. I was a fat kid, and I was more interested in getting candy. I didn't want to waste time and money on tossing toilet paper over trees, spraying shaving cream on cars, and that sort of thing. I just wanted to spend as much time as I could getting as much candy as I could, filling up that damn pillowcase. That was a fat kid's Halloween. It was probably also the most exercise I got all year, walking all over our neighborhoods. So, I have a warm-and-fuzzy memory of what Halloween was all about.

Each of us has a demographic we identify with. I'm not going to force you to be categorized into your age demo. If you self-identify as a tween, no matter how old you are, then, by all means, please do so. Since I've had the great pleasure of working on haunted attractions for each of these demographics, I thought it would be fun to break it down and talk about the individual needs of each one. Each level requires different stuff.

Halloween Events for Kids

Let's start with kids. If you're doing a haunted attraction for the wee ones, that's great. I think it's really important, because it trains the next generation of hauntgoers, it keeps Halloween a vibrant holiday, and it's something families can do together no matter how young the kids are.

Now, I don't have kids other than Lucy the Demon Dog, and she won't go trick-or-treating. She just wants to chase cars. So, I have to indulge my kid side by working on kid events.

Years ago, I did a little bit of work with SeaWorld Spooktacular, which is a wonderful, child-focused event. It's all based on fantasy under the ocean, because it was at SeaWorld. It was a ton of fun for toddlers. I've also done some work with Tampa's Lowry Park Zoo on their Halloween events over the years and written animal shows for them. They're straddling two different demographics, kids and tweens, and they wanted to keep as much kid-friendly stuff in their experience as possible, because that's their target demo during the day. They do great with the stroller moms, so they didn't want to lose that when they went into the night product.

Dress-up and Pretend

SeaWorld was focusing on fun, fantasy, pretend, dress-up, and fairytales—that side of Halloween, which is the purest and simplest. It's so much fun to walk around an event like Spooktacular, which is now called Creatures of the Night, and see these little guys pretending. A little girl walks around the corner and sees a fairy or a princess, and her eyes light up. Better yet, she's dressed like a fairy or a princess—or he is. Who am I to assign gender roles to people? For those who know me, I'm nowhere near a guy to assign gender roles to people. These kids have these moments of pretend and dress-up, and they're so into it. When a kid puts on a Halloween costume for the first time and goes out there, they actually become those characters. They're not just wearing clothes that look like those characters, they *are* the characters.

If you're developing a Halloween event for kids, for that age demographic, include elements that give them places to do creative play. Give them places to live as those fantasy characters they're dressed up as. You can throw in moments of a playful scare. One of the things I love to do with little-kid events is to put hidden audio that makes it sound like there are either trolls or playful critters hiding in the bushes. There's nothing that jumps out, but there will be a voice that says, "Hey, over here." The kids will look and try to find it, and it becomes this sort of game of hide-and-seek. I guess that's kind of cruel on my part, because they're never going to find anything. It gives them a playful scare, and it lets their imagination kick in.

Again, being a kid who grew up trick-or-treating, I think candy has to be an essential element in any child-targeted Halloween event. It's always fun to get something for nothing, whether it's at trick-or-treat or trunk-or-treat or going out to different candy stations at a zoo, aquarium, or museum. If it's a kids' event, you gotta do candy. However, because we have parents out there who are concerned about their children's health—as well they should be, because they're parents—there should also be healthy alternatives—but, obviously, never anything with peanuts (the allergy thing).

Have Something for the Older Siblings

A challenge with doing a kids-only event is that families often have more than the tiny toddler munchkins. Usually, there are older brothers and sisters who want to come along, and that kind of bridges you into the tween audience. So, you have to have something that's at least compelling enough to keep the 11-year-old girl from rolling her eyes and saying, "Oh my God," or the 11-year-old boy from texting his friend, "This is so lame." You have to have a couple of things in there that are cool to look at. They don't necessarily need to be terrifying, but they need to be visually compelling or technologically advanced, so those older kids have things to look at or do.

Don't Go Totally Dark

Another consideration with kids' events is the dark factor. These events aren't as dark as adult events, from a lighting standpoint, because kids are afraid of the dark. I've seen more kids not go into a haunted house because it's dark than not go into a haunted house because there's a giant hulking monster with an ax. Little ones are very much afraid of the dark, so keep that in mind. If you're going to do a kid-friendly event, instead of doing dark, replace it with saturated lighting. Even blacklight works. Do something with really dark jewel tones, so it has playfulness, it has fantasy, and you're giving them the bridge into something that's going to be darker. Also, make sure your scenic and costumes are richly detailed, because they're going to be seen longer and in brighter light, and the kids aren't going to be running away from them.

A Haybale Adventure

Another idea that SeaWorld used to do that I thought was really fun is a haybale maze. They created a maze out of haybales that didn't have a top on it and that grownups could see over. The adventurous little kids could go through on their own, and Mom and Dad could always see the little ones walking through the maze. There were cutouts of whatever characters happened to be in the maze—goofy monsters or whatever. SeaWorld had Sesame Street characters in their Halloween costumes, which were two-dimensional cutouts that the kids would discover as they walked around a corner. This is a training maze, a place to play, and it reinforces the idea that kids who are dressed up can have some creative character play while they're at that Halloween event.

HALLOWEEN EVENTS FOR TWEENS

The next group I want to talk about is the tweens. I call this group the eye-rollers. If you have tweens, you know what I'm talking about. It's a very brief demographic phase. They think they're ready for absolutely everything horror and haunt has to offer—and some of them are, quite honestly. But most of them aren't and, more importantly, unless they're a tween in the haunt community and have been raised doing haunted houses, their parents don't think they're ready. It's Mom and Dad that are footing the bill for these kinds of haunted attractions, so you have to make certain you give them a little bit more and something creepy.

Ghosts—Yes. Gore—Not So Much.

Ghosts are always good, monsters are always good, but I'd keep the gore to a minimum for tweens. It's okay to have the threat of a monster coming out, and you can do a few boo scares, a few startle scares, but don't go over the top. The 11-year-old thinks they want the chainsaw and the ax murders and the blood spurting out everywhere. Some 11-year-olds are great with that, and I know some 30-year-olds that aren't too cool with it. Generally speaking, for the tweens, keep it to monsters.

I actually like using urban legends for this demographic. Ghost stories work really well. I think Slender Man would be kinda cool or things tweens have seen online, games they've played, and that kind of thing. I realize that 11- and 12-year-olds have played games we could never recreate in three dimensions, because we'd need a mop and a drain system. I get that. But I think you also have to play to the parents' sensibilities as well. Give them something startling but not over-the-top gory. Also, if you're dealing with tweens, keep sexuality to a minimum, because, well… just do it. It's a lot safer for everybody involved.

How About Z-tag?

One thing that's fun for the tween audience is Gantom Lighting's Z-tag. This is basically a giant, interactive, zombie game that uses pin-on badges that light up different colors. You can either be a zombie, a human, or a doctor. If you're a human and stand in front of a zombie for more than 15 seconds from three feet away or less, your light starts to flash. This means you can be transformed into a zombie unless you find a doctor who can cure you. It becomes this interactive game where people run all over your event. I think it's cool enough for the tweens, or, at least, it gives them something cool to do at a kids' event while their little brothers and sisters are waving at the pirates and fairies.

Halloween Events for Teens—plus

Now, we're going to get into why so many people love to live in the haunt industry, which is the demographic I call teens-plus. The teens-plus are the 16-, 17-, 18-year-olds all the way up to—well, for me, it's probably going to be all the way up until death. This is where you can really go for it and push that envelope. This is where the majority of independent haunts are, and they really, really go for it.

Deliver the Unexpected

When you go for it, that doesn't mean be as bloody as you can be. It means giving guests something they don't expect. It's Halloween, and you're out to scare people. If guests expect certain things and you deliver those, that isn't scary nor does it give them that adrenaline rush they're looking for. Make sure you do something unique and clever, a little bit over the top, and you're not just setting up the same rooms everybody has seen. I won't go into the importance of story or the importance of having the story build and then have some sort of falling action, because you've heard me say this way too often. What I will say is, make sure you get to this audience on a visceral, emotional level. Flip the script, and do something unexpected.

There was an idea we had at Busch Gardens that never quite got off the ground. I'll throw it out there in case anybody wants to try it someday. Do an upgrade experience where guests are picked up at their house in a hearse and arrive at your haunt in a hearse. If you really want to go there, put them in a coffin. These kinds of things may sound crazy, but there's a phrase I've been using a lot recently: "The shortest path to mediocrity is practicality, so don't be mediocre." Raise your highs to an 11 on a scale of 10, and people will remember your haunted attraction with fondness and terror. So, raise the bar.

For this teens-plus age group, it's okay to be a little bit sexy. Sensuality has always been in horror films and in the haunt industry—and not just backstage in the dressing rooms. You haunters know exactly what I'm talking about. It's always been part of the genre, so it's okay to include that.

Halloween Events for Adults

For this demographic, Halloween means a night out. We're at the mid-range, where people are in their thirties, they've got a babysitter for the kids, and they're going out with their friends. This is the demographic everybody understands the most. They may have had a couple cocktails before arriving, and they'll probably have dinner either before or after visiting your haunt, so you want to scare the living crap out of them. Do something they'll remember. Make it a full experience. Don't just set up some black walls and have a few monsters running around, because that ain't gonna cut it. If you do something completely strange and unexpected, you'll create loyalty, and they'll come back year after year. If you screw it up, you've got one shot and then they're gone.

I've discovered there's definitely a market for the more mature hauntgoer. These are folks who want some form of elegant fear. It was a great experience to do the different years of The Vault of Souls, and I know there are still people out there who experienced that event and continue to ask me, "Is it coming back? When is it coming back? How can we do something like this?" There are a few places out there that offer this kind of thing, but it was something that was very, very special. Who knows? I can't predict the future. We'll see whether it's coming back someday in the future. If it does, I hope I'm involved, because it was an awful lot of fun. Did we do everything absolutely right in the The Vault of Souls? No, probably not, but we did please a lot of guests and gave them an experience they've never had anywhere else. So, keep that in mind.

This Group Wants Psychological Fear

If you're approaching a grown-up, more mature audience, you can raise your price point a little bit, because they're at a place in their life where they have that income to spend on a posh night out. I always say dial down the gore and startle, because, again, usually by the time people have gotten to this point in their haunted-attraction progression, they're like, "Yeah, been there done that. Drop doors just give me a headache now. Strobe lights? No." Psychological fear—things that make them think, things that make them feel something, ghosts, and paranormal—works well with this age group, as does giving them something to do or figure out.

Include Food and Cocktails

I'd also strongly recommend that you include food, cocktails, and a place to start and end the night. One of the things that grew out of The Vault of Souls is a place called CW's Gin Joint, which was the last "act" of The Vault of Souls. It was a 1920s gin joint, and it's now a well-received restaurant in downtown Tampa.

Now, I'm not taking credit for that in any way, shape, or form. That's all the Wilson Company—specifically, Caroline Wilson, who stepped in and brought together the most amazing team of bartenders, an executive chef, and invested beaucoup bucks into creating this beautiful environment. It's unique, and it was that uniqueness that we had the chance to test out in The Vault of Souls. It continues to be a ridiculously popular restaurant here in Tampa. So, if you have the opportunity to dine at CW's Gin Joint, do it, but you need a reservation, because they're full almost every night. This is the kind of thing the grown-up Halloween folks certainly gravitate to.

Decide on Your Target Audience, and Commit to It

You might think I'm going to say, "I think everybody should target this or that demographic." No, I'm not going to say that at all. You need to find what's right for you, what works with your space, your passion, your dollars and cents, and your audience. All I'm going to say is, decide which of these four audiences you want to serve, and commit to it.

Commit to it, because you can't be everything to everyone. You can't try to create an event that has a kiddy thing here, a tween thing here, an over-the-top teen-plus thing here, and an adult thing here. If you attempt to do this, what will happen is you won't be able to communicate through marketing what your event is all about, so you'll always be disappointing someone. You may think, "If I'm all things to all people, I'll have a broader demographic." No. If you try to be all things to all people, you're nothing to anyone. You have to decide to be the best haunted Halloween experience for stroller moms and their toddlers that you can possibly be. If you want to go over the top and be bloody and gory, go over the top and be bloody and gory, but don't try to dumb it down for kids.

What about No–scare Amulets and Lights–on Nights?

People ask me about things like the no-scare amulet. Everyone has their own opinion on these. Basically, this is either a glow stick or a necklace—or some places use wands or amulets—that identifies a child—or even an adult—that chooses not to be scared. My opinion on these is, don't do them, and here's why: As somebody who wants to be scared when I come to these events, if I'm in a group with a person who has a no-scare amulet, it makes the actors timid. It makes them not give me the product I want from the experience. It doesn't give me the scare I'm looking for. The result is, it disappoints the people who are there to be scared.

Then there are things like a kids' night or a lights-on night. I have mixed feelings about these. I understand why people do it, but I think the biggest concern is that the majority of audience members don't read. Say you do this at the end of your season. Somebody shows up expecting your full-blown show, and you give them a brighter-light tour to ramp down the fear. If you've been a full-scare house through the whole season, you run the risk of people not getting it and thinking, "Well, that was kinda lame." There are haunts that do this every year, but, like I said, I have mixed feelings. I think you need to make a choice, target your audience, stick to it, and be the best you can.

Instead, Ramp Up the Fear

Instead of dumbing down or pulling back the fear for certain audiences on certain nights or having amulets or necklaces that protect them, I'd suggest going the other route. There's a haunt here in Florida called Screamageddon. It's a full-contact haunt if you're wearing a glow necklace, which means they're not dumbing down the scare, they're ramping it up. They're giving someone an opportunity to be even more involved, more scared. A lot of haunts do lights-out. As I mentioned earlier, there's one haunt—in England, I think—where guests go through a totally dark haunt naked on their closing night. That really takes it to the next quirky level. Would I do it? Oh, hell yeah! My biggest fear would be going through the house without my clothes on and finding my clothes are gone when I'm done. A naked-guest haunt is a great talking point, and a great way to get return visits. They've created a haunt that people love, is top notch, and guests have the chance to do something that's really brag-worthy.

I think you should ramp up the fear. Do a flashlight tour the last night. If you've got a really detailed haunt, turn all your lighting off and hand people flashlights. Let them go through in the dark, keep all your actors out there, and scare the snot out of them. Raise the bar rather than dumb it down—and, most importantly, if you do that, make sure you communicate everything clearly.

What I've been trying to say in this section is good Halloween is good for Halloween. Good haunts are good for the haunt industry. Whether you're a kiddie, stroller-mom fantasy haunt; an extreme haunt; or an adult, elegant-fear night out, do it to the best of your ability, and don't try to be everything to everyone. If you're laser focused, you'll be able to make choices based on what's best for your haunt, not what's best for your wallet. I promise you, if you start to think that way, you'll actually lose money.

At a haunt I worked at years ago—and you'll probably figure out which one when I start telling this story—our guests told us early on, "If you're going to offer things for my kids, don't make it a nighttime event.

You're open until midnight or one o'clock, so, if you're going to do stuff that's scary, do stuff that's scary, but don't have the goofy mascot kind of characters roaming around. Make a decision." Choose your market, stick to your guns, market correctly, and make sure everybody—no matter what age—has something to do, something that's fun, and a way to celebrate the Halloween season.

PART TWO

GUTS AND BOLTS: OPERATIONS 101

Chapter 7

SET YOUR DIRECTION, AND COMMUNICATE IT

The key to creating a great haunt is communication throughout the whole process—from creation to installation. In this chapter, I'm going to talk about how to communicate between creatives and directors and directors and producers—you know, the people who have the money—and how to pitch new ideas. Also, I recently did a great interview with scenic designer and educator Chris Kleckner, and highlights from that are included here, too. I'll also be talking about a terrific new book that will help you with brainstorming. It's called *The Event Brainstormer* and was written by Bob Glickman.

THE CHALLENGE

So, I'm going to start by talking about communication in general. In this industry, you need to communicate with a whole bunch of different people in different ways. In my position, I often have to communicate with somebody I don't know—a person who has a brand-new project they want me to work on. They give me bits and pieces, and I have to figure out how to share what I can do for them. Then, after the project is approved and I'm working on it, I have to communicate with their designers—or select designers to work with—and figure out who can I communicate with the best. I have to communicate with the other folks who are on my level of the corporate hierarchy. I have to find ways to communicate with the marketing people, the merchandise people, and the culinary people, if those are part of the project. And I have to be able to communicate with the cast. I have to find out how to translate the artistic vision that either I've developed or is being interpreted by me and communicate that to the front-line performers.

Determine Your Goals, and Learn How to Translate Them

I've discovered over the years that communication is kind of tough. It's challenging, because you can't talk to everybody in the same language or give them the same information. I found that the easiest way for me to do this is to figure out, first off, what goals my client is trying to accomplish. In fact, when I do new proposals for anything, this is one of the first things on the written document—what are the goals of this project? Maybe those goals are to terrify the most guests or entertain the most guests or earn the most money or make the facility the star so it can be a marketing tool for other things. All of these are valid goals, but you have to identify what goal you're addressing depending on who you're talking to.

For example, the marketing person's goal is to get as many people through the door as possible. The artistic director's or creative director's goal is usually to create the most amazing event they possibly can—the most artistically interesting and challenging. The producer's goal, as the person who signs the checks, may be to make as much money as possible. The front-line actor's goal may be to have the most fun and scare the most people. So, by identifying and talking about those goals, you're able to figure out what words, what phrases, what things you can bring to the forefront.

Now, once I've done that, most of my job as a communicator during the planning and installation of an event is to act as the translator. I serve as the translator between the producer or client and the actors to let them know that the operational side is important. Without that operational side, they wouldn't have the opportunity to scare people and do what they want to do. So, it's all about making connections among the various goals, and that's actually a lot simpler than it sounds.

First, you want to make certain everybody understands what's important to this group of people, what's important to that group of people, and what's important to you. These goals may all be different. It's vitally important to recognize what's important to each individual and be able to synergize and make connections among all the powers that be and all the elements within any production. Otherwise, you run the risk of things being siloed and having a bunch of ivory towers operating next to each other.

Emphasize the Importance of Collaboration

Another way to think of it is like a shopping mall. Every store has its own goal, but, when they work together, they create an overall shopping experience. The same is true of a haunted attraction—or any performance element, really. It's a collaborative effort. You have to make certain the whole is greater than the sum of the individual parts, and that's exactly what happens in a good theatrical production. Hopefully, people can understand that and understand what's important to other people. That will help you choose the language and information you want to share with them.

Set Good Groundwork to Create Win–Win Scenarios

So, how can you apply all this information? Say it's your first year as the director of a theatrical piece or a haunted attraction or whatever. The most important thing for you to do is set good groundwork so you can continue to do this and be profitable for years to come. The more you're able to find ways to communicate that to the rest of your team, the more likely it is they'll be able to help you with it.

If you're an actor, and it's the first time you've worked in a haunted attraction, you need to really listen to the director so you're clear on what their goals are, what they want to accomplish, and what you can do to help them accomplish those goals. In the same way, if you're a director, you have to listen to your actors. If you hear your actors saying, "I just want to get out there and scare people," don't bore them with the business side but make them understand that the more successful they are at scaring people, the more successful the event will be and the happier you and the producer will be. It's basically figuring out how to explain to people how multiple goals can work simultaneously to support each other and create win-win scenarios.

Chris Kleckner on Communication

Now, let's get to the interview I did with Chris Kleckner. Chris is a scenic designer-builder-production-manager sort of dude, an all-around, get-things-done kind of guy. We had this discussion about directors and creatives talking to designers and how they don't always speak the same language. Chris said he'd noticed, from a designer standpoint, that sometimes directors and writers don't always tell you what they're looking for or how they want things done. I asked him, "What's the biggest stumbling block for you when that happens?"

"It's listening to their words and then trying to extrapolate what they actually mean," he replied. "A director has an entire vision of the entire concept of the entire production they're working on, whereas designers spend all their time focusing on one aspect, and their whole world revolves around that one aspect. So, the level of detail from the broad strokes of the director to the fine brush of a designer is sometimes a little difficult to transpose," he explained.

Sometimes, as a director, I know it's hard to focus on all the fine points that a designer needs to know. I'm always a big proponent of presenting the information and then sitting down with the designer to ask questions and talk about it back and forth. I asked Chris if he found this approach helpful or a waste of time.

"It's definitely helpful. The conversation eventually gets reduced as you develop a relationship with the director," he replied. "When you're working with someone for the first time—especially because directors are passionate about what they do, and they're passionate about the projects they work on—it's sometimes hard for them to trust that someone they've never worked with before will approach the project with the same amount of honesty and earnestness as they do. I can definitely understand why they'd have a hard time doing that."

I agree with Chris. It's same with a designer. A designer may want every little detail to be 100%, even if it's something nobody will ever see in a dark haunted attraction. I asked Chris what we can do to make the conversation easier and more efficient between designers and directors. What kinds of information can directors offer to designers to make them inspired to do their job?

Chris responded, "I know what I want as a director, but, also, I've hired a designer for a reason. They've got experience, and I want them to bring their experience to the table. So, I tell them, 'Here's what I'm looking for, but what do you think?' Often that sparks something else, and what we come up with together will be much better than what either one of us would have come up with independently."

I asked Chris what he thought a director could do to get to that place. What kinds things can a director share with a designer to make their respective jobs easier?

Adjectives, Research, and Collaboration

"Sometimes, directors think they know exactly what they want, and that often means pulling out the set they have in their head and putting it on the stage for them. The easiest way to do this is by using adjectives. We may only choose four of those adjectives at the end of the day, but I've never worked on a project where I've had too many adjectives to pull from. We can decide which ones are good and which ones are bad later. I equate this to an actor. An actor brings certain adjectives to the table, and it's the director's job to eventually decide what to keep, what to lose, what to build off of. We have to bring a pile of stuff first, and that's what I like to do," he explained.

"I also do some teaching, and one of the things I have the hardest time teaching students is the importance of research. In the 21st century, research is so much easier than it used to be, but I've never been on a project where I've had too much research. I always have an idea of what I think something looked like in the 1850s, but I need to do that research again and again and again. Every time I do, I find something different. That something may not ever be used in the project, but I put it in my pocket for some later day, because it's going to become useful eventually," said Chris.

"It's critical to have that open conversation and realize the end game of that conversation is the best story possible. If I'm designing what I believe is the best set possible, I've already failed. I want my sets to be so perfect that they go unnoticed by the audience members, because they're involved in the story. I think we sometimes lose that sense of selflessness, and it becomes a competition of ideas amongst other designers—my set needs to be better than your lights or her costumes or her sound—and that's not what we're there to do. We're all there to use what we're good at to tell the story in a way that no one's heard it, seen it, or felt it before. That's why we continue to do live art."

Those of you who've been listening to my podcasts for a while know exactly why I wanted to talk to Chris, because this is exactly what I've been saying. In fact, the moment he mentioned the word "story," I started doing backflips. It's interesting that he mentioned the best set possible. One of my favorite negative critiques was about a theatrical piece in Chicago. The headline was, "Brilliant Set," and then the article stated, "but the actors kept getting in the way." Clearly, the actors weren't very good, but it's not about the set, it's not about the lights, and it's not about the costumes. It's about all of them and how they work together to tell the story.

"If it wasn't, we wouldn't call it a collaborative art," stated Chris.

Exactly. It would be scenic design or costumes for museums. It's collaborative, and it's so important that it remain collaborative. I told Chris I loved his point about it not becoming a battle of my ideas are better than your ideas or my lighting is better than your set. Ultimately, audiences don't care. They want to be transported somewhere else, and everything has to work together seamlessly so that can happen. The more you can share with each other, the better.

I asked Chris to talk about some of the challenges he's experienced, like a situation in which somebody says, "I want it to be this." A friend of mine, who's an actor, told me a story about his experience with a particular director. He said, "The only direction I got from this director was, 'I want you to be mythical.'" Do you know how impossible it is for an actor to be "mythical?" Because who knows what that means. It was an adjective, but it was a crappy adjective. I asked Chris about direction he's gotten in the past that he didn't know how to interpret.

"From a designer's perspective, it's always, 'I want the elements to float in space,' and builders always want doors without walls or the doors to be skewed or not have the hinges at a right angle. I have to say, 'I'm sorry, the doors don't work that way.' I have to be honest," he said.

Well, I have to say right here that I'm guilty of the, "I want doors without walls." I did have a designer who got pretty close. It required a welder, and he basically put the doors on a heavy metal base plate, welded a frame, and put wood around it. But it was a trip hazard.

"Oftentimes, directors are so caught up in the imaginative that they forget we need to ground some of our thoughts in reality, at least to give us a jumping-off point. It's hard for a diver to dive without a springboard. So, once we have that diving board, we can do things like flips in the air or land without a splash—but, we need the diving board and the water first," Chris noted.

Use Science to Create Fantasy

Chris mentioned the challenge of pulling the set out of the director's head. That's a great idea—except there's no science in the director's imagination. You have to deal with the realities. For example, lighting designers will tell you, "I can't bend the light to go around that set piece. It's going to cast a shadow." Audio designers will say, "No, I can't put a shutter on the speaker so you only hear it when you're standing here but not here." We have to always work within the realms of science and reality to create fantasy.

Chris remarked, "On the flip side, as a designer, I want the director to tell me everything they'd love to have. I tell them we don't have enough time to do all of it, we don't have enough money to do all of it, and we don't have enough resources to do all of it, but directors can sometimes limit themselves by only thinking about what's possible. I don't want a director to have to do that. We might miss a great opportunity, because I may have solved that problem years ago. We may be able to make things happen that they might not have had experience with. So, I want to hear all that information, and then we'll worry about how we're going to pay for it, find the manpower, and what we'll need to strip away to make it possible," he said.

"When my students first do a sketch for a design, I tell them they have an unlimited amount of money, unlimited amount of time, and unlimited amount of manpower, so go design. They'll have to redesign later, but it's important to get those ideas down first, because they might be missing out on the best of their six ideas if they believe they can't afford it."

Bad Ideas Often Spark Great Ideas

And we all know that bad ideas often spark really good ideas. I agree with Chris that you don't want to edit yourself. That's part of the rules of brainstorming—never negate, never say no. One of my favorite lighting designers, a gentleman who's also named Chris, offers the advice that after you've finished your lighting design, take away 50% of your cues. You don't have to leave them all out, but, this way, you get it down to what's essential. If you have to add some back, great, but you'll more than likely have a much more coherent lighting design without any of the floofy, unnecessary, distracting stuff, because everything you need is there. Then, you can go back and add one or two of the other things.

"Selective focus is important, but we don't have to tell audiences where to look every single moment. People are pretty smart," said Chris. "As a builder, I'm pretty good, because I know thousands of things that don't work, and I've allowed myself to try them first. Eventually, I come up with what does work, but it's good to make mistakes and be okay with making mistakes."

Indeed, the only thing that teaches us is failure, so we have to make those mistakes. You don't know bad music until you hear bad music. You have to put yourself out there and allow yourself to stumble and fail, so you can learn from that. You either learn you shouldn't do that again or, if you do it again, you're not going to do it the same way. You can check off one way that doesn't work and see if you can find another 50 that do.

Chris agreed. "Maybe it's not even as stark as what works and what doesn't: 'I did this, and it wasn't the most efficient way to do it.' There could have been a cleaner way to do it. At the other end of the process of self-critiquing your own work constantly, you realize that, just because it's done well, that doesn't mean it's important. That's a hard skill to teach students."

That's a hard skill to teach anyone. It takes time and experience to be able to say, "This could have been better, and that's okay."

"I've never worked on a show that I wouldn't love to revisit and correct," said Chris. "I can look at anything in my past and see a missed opportunity that I'm looking at with fresh eyes. That doesn't mean it was a failure as a design or as a production, but, being able to step away and look at it, you'll always see something that could have been tweaked just a little bit more or finessed just a little bit more gracefully. It's wonderful to be able to view your own stuff in a sort of postmortem sense, because it humbles you for the next project. I actually love to look for ways to do that, because the more humble I become in what I do, the more honest the story is that I'm trying to tell."

I agree with Chris that the more humble you become, the more honest you're able to be and the more each project is about the story and not about you. I'm a huge proponent of people who are confident enough in their work to step out of the way of it.

"Even with fine artists, it's not about them," noted Chris. "It's about their canvas, their sculpture, or whatever their medium is, and that's how it should be for us. It's about the story. It's always about the story. It's never about the lead actor, it's never about the classically trained director, it's never about any of us. We're simply the vehicle. Somewhere along the line, someone has deemed this story to be worth telling in a different way, and there's a reason for that in this time and place, and we should all just work toward that."

The Event Brainstormer—an Invaluable Tool for Generating Ideas

And now let's get back to our theme of different people having different ways of communicating. I think Chris brought up some excellent points, one of which was brainstorming. Brainstorming is an often-forgotten but essential part of the development of a new project or even polishing an existing project. The idea behind brainstorming is basically to throw as many ideas onto the table as possible. I have a friend who refers to it as "dating ideas rather than marrying them." Throw out as many cool ideas as possible, and don't throw anything off the table yet. Chris mentioned not worrying about budget or anything else, because the best idea, or the one that sparks the coolest idea, might be the one that's the most ridiculously expensive.

In addition to doing brainstorming with your own team, it's important to have tools and resources to help you. Like I said, I'm all about research, and Chris mentioned the importance of research, too. And that brings us back to *The Event Brainstormer* by Bob Glickman. It's available on Amazon. The book's blurb says, "Keep your events fresh, engaging, and successful with over 800 creative concepts and elements for the event professional." This is not, by any stretch of the imagination, a book on how to start your brand-new event-planning-and-producing business. It's not that. It's brainstorming in a nutshell. What Mr. Glickman has done is put together list upon list of ideas, with themes, entertainment options, and scenic elements arranged in alphabetical order to not only polish the ideas you may have but to spark new ideas for whatever event you happen to be doing.

The reason I think this is so important to haunters is that we're basically putting together an event—a seasonal festival. The more you can make it unique, different, and exciting, the more successful you're going to be. Maybe you're thinking about adding something. You may want to sit down, brainstorm, and figure out what you can or should add. Should you add different kinds of queue entertainment? Should you add different scenics? Can you do an off-season party with a specific theme? There are all kinds of ideas and opportunities in this book.

The layout of *The Event Brainstormer* makes it amazingly easy to use—beginning with, Introduction: How to Use this Book. It's then broken down into overarching event themes—everything from a time-period theme to a music theme to an athletic theme. Creative elements are broken down into scenery, performers, entertainment experiences, ideas for costuming, etc. Finally, there are the technical elements—audio, lighting, video, special effects, and that kind of thing. It doesn't explain to you how Glickman Productions, which is the author's company, works, but it shares his years and years of experience. It's an encyclopedia of what he's tried and what's worked for him. It can save you a lot of time and energy, not to mention really spark creative ideas for new events, for new elements, for new parties, or whatever.

If you're in the haunt industry or the special-events industry, you're already a professional events planner or producer, so I strongly recommend picking up this book. It's not very long—about 60-some pages, paperback—but it will save you tremendously in labor. You don't have to hire someone to come in and brainstorm with you or facilitate brainstorming.

Chapter 8

Sound Makes a Difference

This chapter is all about audio and why it's a key element in the development of your attraction. Audio completes your haunt environment and makes it real, so it's important to get it right.

Gone are the days of setting up your haunt and getting a CD of that "ooooaaaaa" sound that every single ghost animation used to make. Those of you who are laughing right now know exactly what I'm talking about—every animation and every vibrating ghost on a string used that one sound chip.

Sound Is Essential to Bring Guests Completely into Your World

I'm not a tech guy or an audio designer, but I've had the opportunity to work with a lot of really cool audio folks, and I've picked up some tips along the way. First and foremost, if you're going to do a haunt, you have to find somebody who knows how to incorporate sound. I know many people think haunts are a visual medium and that should be the main focus, but guests need to hear the experience as well. Sound creates a sense of reality. Whether it's music, sound effects, or even sounds made by the actors, it's important to recognize that audio completes your environment and makes it real. No matter where you are, sound impacts the way you feel about where you are. Even when it's completely silent—or you think it's completely silent—there's always something in the background.

Here's an example. We did a haunted house many, many years ago that was set in a subway, and I wanted the sound of a subway throughout the entire house—the sound of cars rattling overhead, the trains in the background—because it provided that ambient depth to the environment. Your brain tricks you into thinking you aren't in a warehouse or wherever. That haunt was actually in the old bumper-cars location at Busch Gardens Tampa. So, I wanted to transport guests with that ambient sound to complete the mood.

Sound Makes a Space Seem Larger and Enhances the Scares

A lot of people don't realize this, but sound makes a space seem larger. If you hear something you don't see—something that's coming from outside the location you're in—it creates the sense of a whole world out there beyond the world of your haunted attraction and the queue line. It's the world of the particular story you're trying to tell in your haunt. This sounds weird, but incorporating audio makes that world bigger, so you want to add sound outside the room.

Of course, sound enhances the scares. We're going to talk about all of this in greater detail with specific suggestions and ideas as we go along. Sound enhances the scares in several ways, such as building a sense of anticipation. Movies have known this for years. You hear the fright fiddles and the horror horns, and those are used to build a sense of anticipation: "Don't open that door! Don't walk around that corner!" Audio can also be used to reinforce and enhance a visual scare, a drop door, a character emerging into a pool of light. Let's face it, if you clap your hands loud enough in a quiet room, people are going to jump, so don't underestimate the power of audio as a real scare tactic.

Of course, I'm not going to get through this or any topic without talking about how important storytelling is. You can use audio to help convey the details of your story. One thing I've done in several haunted attractions is have a radio playing in one of the scenes. Sometimes, the broadcast is directly about the storyline of the haunt itself—for example, a police alert saying, "Be on the lookout for X, Y, or Z." Sometimes, it's just music playing from the era or location of the storyline to enhance that sense of reality. You can do this with a radio or television or a phone hanging off the hook. You could have a little speaker in the phone receiver and have somebody screaming out through the receiver, "George, where are you? We were just talking. George! GEORGE!" It draws people in and, again, it helps tell that story.

Audio Turns Your Haunt into a Horror Film

The most important reason to incorporate audio—and I mean audio on a grand scale—is it makes your haunt more like a horror film. Most people who go to haunted attractions have been to a horror film. They've seen scary movies, so it's important to give them that same experience, only live. Live theater, live performance, is always in 3D, whereas movies are 2D—except for the ones where you wear the special glasses. A haunt breaks down that barrier between the audience and the film. We're trying to create a movie that guests walk through and get scared in. Without incorporating audio—whether it's music, sound effects, or whatever—you've lost one whole element. And people recognize it right off the bat. As guests exit your haunt, they'll be thinking, "Hey, there was no music. There wasn't any sound in there." Whether they're aware of it or not, they won't have nearly the rich experience they would if music and sound effects had been incorporated. In a nutshell, if you don't include sound, you're missing out on a very important element of the storytelling.

Create an Underscore

Now I'd like to focus on the idea of an underscore or a music bed versus what I call point-source or specific locations that emanate sound of some kind. Using an underscore will definitely reinforce the mood.

We've already talked about how audio makes your haunt world seem bigger. There was a haunted attraction we did at Howl-O-Scream that was called Catch Your Breath. In Catch Your Breath, we were able to use audio in a lot of different ways, and I'll give you a couple examples. The idea of the haunt was that it took place in a small rural town and there was a motorcycle gang that would kill 13 people in this town on the 13th of every October. Each time they killed someone, they'd leave a dead dove beside the body. Each year, we'd have a different murder theme. It started with Catch Your Breath, in which all the victims were suffocated.

Since it was a rural town, we had Patsy Cline playing in the queue. Now, I'm sorry if you're a Patsy Cline fan, but I think Patsy Cline can be kinda creepy, especially if you make it scratchy. We were lucky enough to be working with a theme park that was BMI-ASCAP licensed, so we could use pretty much anything as long as we reported it and paid a ton of money to make it happen. We'll talk more about licensing a little later. I'm clearly not an expert, but I'll tell you what I know and give you some ideas about where to look to find answers about licensing as opposed to hiring a lawyer. So, we had Patsy Cline music playing in the queue, which took you to a certain era in this small rural town.

Another thing I used as an underscore or sound bed was the sound of doves cooing—which, to me, sounds kind of ghostly. Of course, this was part of the story in that, at every murder scene, there was a dead dove left by this motorcycle gang. I wanted that ghostly, creepy sound of doves cooing throughout the entire house, and it set people on edge.

An underscore can also help focus guests' attention. It acts as a distraction to any outside noise. When the dove noises were playing inside the house, guests couldn't hear the people in the queue or the music that was happening outside. It created almost a white-noise effect. This will work in pretty much any haunted house. If you have a music bed, it brings guests' focus into the space itself. In one of our houses, we tried to do a music bed of creaking wood and whispers that faded from one side of the house to the other. This sounded really cool on paper, but it wasn't noticeable in the house. Standing in one location, it sounded like the volume went up and down, but it was actually shifting from one side of the house to the other. We had much better success doing the exact same thing in a single room. For example, we did a boathouse scene in one of our haunted houses, and the boathouse actually rocked like it was floating on water. We faded the lapping and creaking slightly from one side to the other to match the rocking of the boathouse. Using that kind of audio really reinforced the reality by putting our guests specifically in that location. It didn't matter if they were hearing anything before or after. That sound masked any subtle noises and made it work really well.

Use Sound to Heighten Suspense

Of course, the most important reason to use any sort of sound or music in a haunted attraction is to create suspense. If you've ever watched an Alfred Hitchcock movie, you know he was amazing at using music to create suspense. Even movies that, in my opinion, weren't that great, like *Eyes Wide Shut*, used music exceptionally well to set the tone. I know I'll get letters from people saying *Eyes Wide Shut* was the best movie ever, but I didn't care for it. However, it did use music effectively, and I'd strongly recommend you watch about five or 10 minutes of that film to see how they used that single bing, bing to great effect. The music was minimalistic, which really set the tone beautifully and created suspense. You were always wondering what was going to happen next in that film—even though the answer was, "very little." So, use the underscore to create suspense.

Use Point–Source Audio to Draw Guests' Attention

I mentioned point-source audio, and I'll explain what that is. With underscoring or a music bed, the sound seems to be coming from the entire room. This is achieved by placing a few speakers around the room to create an even coverage of the sound. Point-source audio comes from a specific location and is usually done with a smaller speaker or a noisemaker that an actor holds. The purpose is to give the sense that the sound is coming from one specific location.

Use point-source audio to help focus where guests should look. Say you have a queue actor who's on a microphone. Put the speakers near where the queue actor is standing, so his voice isn't coming from behind the guests—which is just weird and distracting in the wrong way. If you use point-source well, it enhances the scares. If you put a triggered scream on a drop door, you've got this amazing, voice-saving audio device that works really, really well. If you use point-source audio as a distraction to draw people's attention in one direction, all the guests will be looking at that spot, which gives the actors the opportunity to scare them from the other side of the room or from behind.

Going back to Catch Your Breath, in the very first room, we had a pay phone that was ringing non-stop. Now, if you're too young to remember what an actual ringing phone sounds like, it's not a chirp, it's not the theme from Star Wars, it's none of that. It's actually a ringing sound, and it's really, really annoying after a long period of time. We had this incessant ringing coming directly from a pay phone that was hanging on the wall. I just realized, pay phones are probably something many people haven't seen, either. Anyway, look it up. This ringing not only put people on edge, but it also acted as a distraction, because everybody was looking at this phone, so the performers in the room could scare from behind.

Point-Source Audio Enhances the Realism

The other thing about point-source audio—and the same is true for point-source lighting—is it makes the room seem real. If there's a radio in the room, the sound should be coming only from the radio. If you've got a blender in a kitchen scene, and there's a hand sticking out of the top and swirling around inside the blender, there should be a sound coming from a speaker placed underneath that blender, not from speakers all around the room. If you've got a birdcage and you want the sound of birds coming from the birdcage, make sure the speaker is there.

Our audio designer used point-source audio really cleverly at Howl-O-Scream. We created a scare zone in which we took two stereo tracks and cranked all the source to one side and then all the source to the other. We wanted our guests to feel like they were being watched by a bunch of little trolls and creepy monsters living in the bushes, so we put speakers in the bushes. If we hadn't taken the stereo system and cranked it from one side to the other, it would have been considered a music bed. But, since we did, only a certain voice came out of one speaker and, later, that same voice would come out of another speaker, so it would create the illusion you were being followed, because the speakers were staggered. The audio was very simple. We recorded somebody saying, "Look, they're coming. Look over here, look over here." We'd get people to start looking through the bushes trying to find them. On the next track would be, "Ah, you didn't find us. We got ahead of you. We see you."

In this way, we used audio as a character. If you've got a voice coming from one specific source and then that same voice coming from another source, it becomes like a moving character. Anybody can do this who has GarageBand or Audacity, and you can use very simple ideas and materials to create point-source scares. The key is having the sound come from the speaker at the source—underneath the birdcage, inside the crate where the growling demon is held, etc. This not only makes sense from a realism standpoint but allows you to focus guests' attention.

Audio Equipment Doesn't Need to Be Expensive

Now I'm going to talk about audio equipment in very general terms, because I'm not an audio guy. First of all, audio equipment doesn't need to be expensive. If you've got one audio system to play your bed or whatever your underscoring is going to be, you can use things like portable MP3 players or even a portable CD player. You can hook these up to little Bluetooth speakers, and those are more than enough for point-source audio. If there's a scratchy old radio playing in the corner, number one, it doesn't need to be high-fidelity sound, and, number two, it only needs to play quietly from a corner. If it's super loud, it's going to fill the whole room. There are all kinds of tiny speakers out there for very little money at places like Walmart, Target, and those kinds of stores.

If you're able to have a centrally controlled audio system, that's a huge advantage. You can control everything from one location. You don't have to go to every speaker and adjust the levels. Obviously, this is more expensive, but it does give you significantly more control. Another huge advantage of having centralized control is that if something goes wrong in the house and you have to shut it down, you have a God mic, which is basically a microphone that allows you to talk to the entire house or broadcast an emergency announcement like, "Ladies and gentlemen, it's time to evacuate the house. Please move to the nearest exit," or whatever.

If you're working in a haunted attraction in a historic site or someplace with stone walls, you may not be able or allowed to drill holes in the walls to run cables to speakers. You may have to go with independently powered or even battery-powered smaller units to create your audio experience.

Design Your Haunt for the Equipment You Have

People are always saying, "I'm so jealous. I wish I had X, Y, or Z piece of equipment." The grass is always greener—or the haunt is always scarier—in somebody else's yard. What you really need to focus on is designing for the equipment you have. If you've got eight boomboxes, three MP3 players, and your grandma's old stereo, don't design a haunt that requires a symphonic overture to be played anywhere, because it's going to sound tinny and not good. However, if you decide to design a haunt in which you're chasing cannibalistic homeless people through a junkyard, well, looky there, your equipment is perfect for that. Sometimes, low production value can be your friend. That scratchiness in the source material or in the speaker itself can work really well, and you don't have to pay anybody to add it.

However, if you have the opportunity to work in an audio studio, take it. I'm not going to lie to you and say, "I'd much prefer to record things on my phone and play them back over an MP3 player that's connected to a $15 speaker I got at Walmart." No, I wouldn't prefer that, but you can make it work. I realize not a whole lot of readers have access to a professional studio, but you can always buy studio time and work that into your budget. It's not a bad idea in some cases, but you can also find ways to do it cheaper. Digital recording is now something pretty much anybody can do. It takes a little bit of study, and you need somebody who can operate the equipment with GarageBand or Audacity. You can even get Pro Tools on your laptop. You can mix and put together a lot of your own stuff.

Work with Your Local University

If you have a college, university, or even a trade school in your area that has an audio or theatrical sound studio, you might be able to get in as a project with a local university. If there are students looking for a final project that involves mixing, recording, editing, and designing for a three-dimensional space, you might only have to pay for studio time—not for the board operator, designer, recording engineer, or any of those things. Again, I'm not trying to NOT pay people, but sometimes there are students out there who need the experience and can't get it anywhere else, and there are haunters out there who need the product and can't get it anywhere else. It never hurts to ask. Create win-win scenarios. You've given this audio-designer dude or gal a great opportunity to design something they wouldn't have had the opportunity to do otherwise, and you get something affordable and of higher quality than you could do on your own, because the students are out there trying to make things work and impress their professors. As a little side note, you might get that university to help promote your haunt, so that never hurts, either.

The Value of Triggers

Before I leave the topic of equipment, there's one other thing I want to talk about, and that's triggers. With point-source audio, you don't always want it playing on a loop all the time, so you might consider investing in some inexpensive triggers. There are all kinds of them. Motion triggers start your playback when something comes close to them, and pressure-pad triggers deploy when somebody steps on them. Triggers can be used for audio, animation, or even lighting. A company that offers lots of triggers is Fright Props. I'm not saying they're the only or the best source, I'm saying they're the first one that comes to my mind, because I've used their products before. This is not a paid advertisement, but it's a place to start.

There are some high-end triggers that will rotate and can be used to trigger up to four different audio tracks. One of my favorite uses for triggers is with the bungee apparatus called Slingshot, where the performer jumps out of the darkness and either bounces on the ground, flies out over your head and then bounces back up to a platform in the dark, or just leaps straight off the platform and scares you. At Howl-O-Scream, we added a motion sensor or a proximity trigger so that when the performer broke the beam on this trigger, it deployed an audio sound, which would be a different sound every three or four times the trigger was fired. So, one time the monster coming out would be Scream 1, the next time it would be Scream 2, and the next time it would be Scream 3. The performers got used to the sequence, so they, in turn, would lip-sync to these monster sounds. It saved their voice. Being on a slingshot or a bungee is really exhausting, so if the performers don't have to scream as they come out, it becomes far more impactful. Those speakers were put underneath the platform, so the sound and visuals were coming from the same side of the pathway as where the performers were located.

Sources of Great Haunt Sounds

Whether you've got a multi-bazillion-dollar audio set-up, your five MP3 players, an iPad, or your grandma's old stereo speakers, you have to find something to put on them. Before we get into recorded sound, let's take a little time to talk about something that every haunted attraction has probably used at one time or another—noisemakers used by actors. Back in the day, we used shaker boxes. Shaker boxes are good for beginning haunts, but you need to make them sturdy. I can't tell you how many shaker boxes or shaker cans I've seen at haunted attractions that get smacked up against a wall, break open, and little nuts and bolts fly everywhere. I've also seen actors who bang them into their own fingers. So, make sure those boxes are padded whenever possible, and give the actors gloves whenever possible. That being said, if you can find a way to eliminate using shaker boxes, do that. I don't think they're a great scare. They don't do much for me.

Better than shaker boxes is taking little pieces of metal conduit, cutting them into 8- to 12-inch-long pieces, and wrapping one end with duct tape so it serves as a handle. You can take two of these and bang them together to create this metallic industrial sound, or you can scrape them along the concrete. This works especially well if you have sliders—those guys who run out of the darkness, drop to their protective knee-gear and steel-toed boots, and scare people. If your sliders are dragging these little conduit pipes, not only do they throw off sparks, but they make a horrible sound.

Of course, the be-all and end-all for every single haunt I've ever been to is the chainless chainsaw. I know everybody thinks of that as a prop, but what really makes it scary is the ungodly loud noise. They make some good fake chainsaws now that have speakers in them. The growling comes from the engine, not the blade itself. The other thing about chainsaws that works really well is the smell of the gasoline, but you can only use them outside, or ventilation becomes an issue. I think chainsaws are a little overused, but most haunt guests don't think that. Most haunt guests think they're really, really cool and will expect them as they leave your haunted attraction.

Another great noisemaker out there is a battery-powered car horn hooked up to lights. These work really well if you're doing a clown theme. It's fun to all of a sudden hear a horn blast coming out of the darkness that scares the heck out of you. Shovels also work well as noisemakers. Scraping a shovel across concrete creates a really unnerving, terrifying sound, just like the metal pipes we mentioned earlier.

I've tested many kinds of sounds in my many years of haunting. Goose and duck calls work well with clowns. Tibetan meditation bowls aren't necessarily scary, but they create a really cool atmosphere. They come in various sizes and different tones. We've even gone so far as to test what I call clap gloves. These are basically two pieces of wood that have been epoxied to leather gloves. When the hands are clapped together, it makes a slapping sound. This is actor-generated audio.

I should mention that I never use whistles as audio or sound effects. The reason is that, for many years, whistles have been used to announce there's something wrong or there's an emergency. For the same reason, I'd say a siren would also be a bad idea to use as a scare sound.

Sources of Live and Recorded Music and Sound Effects

Now we're going to talk about where to find sources for music or sound effects that you can either record or use live in your haunts. Before I begin talking about this, I strongly recommend you do some research and find out what you can legally use and what you can't. Different musicians have different requirements, restrictions, and licenses to use their material. I mentioned BMI-ASCAP earlier when I talked about working for Busch Gardens Howl-O-Scream. When I worked at The Vault of Souls, we created our own audio soundtrack, so we didn't have to worry about using outside audio. I wrote a couple of songs, hired musicians, and put them into the studio. So, look into what the rules, regulations, licenses, and laws are for each piece of music you want to use.

Sound Makes a Difference

There are websites that shed some light on this situation. One of them is PDInfo.com, another is FreeMusicArchive.org, and there's another called MakeUseOf.com. All of those will give you insight into what you legally can and cannot use for music. They also have a huge library of public-domain music, which is music by artists who don't want a bazillion dollars every time you play their song. In many cases, this music has a common-use license, which means all you have to do is credit the artist.

For many years, there were people who made music for haunted attractions, and all you had to do was register with them. Midnight Syndicate is one. There are some great haunt musicians that create these beautiful soundtracks for haunted attractions, things that can play in the background. Besides Midnight Syndicate, there's NoxArchana and a relatively new one called Shadows Symphony. Buzzworks is another one. Anybody who's been to any haunted attraction tradeshow knows Midnight Syndicate has a disk for pretty much any theme you'd ever want to use, and they're great guys to work with. You can chat with them, explain what you're trying to do, and make sure you have their blessing to use their music. Let's be honest, everybody who works that hard to create something that wonderful deserves to be compensated in some way, shape, or form.

So, when it comes to using music, make sure you're doing the right thing and following the rules and laws. Breaking the law is going to take a lot of profit out of your haunted attraction. You can try to sneak some music in without going through proper channels, but I don't recommend it. If it does catch up with you, it's going to limit you significantly, and you're not going to be in good shape. My recommendation is to find a few talented musicians, put mixing software on a laptop, and create your own cool soundtrack. It can be just a few chords or a few notes, or it might be a full band. You might even be able to find a local goth and/or creepy band to do something original for you. I don't know if creepy is a music genre. You probably need to pay them a few bucks, but they also may do it just to have their music heard. With the electronic software that's out there, people can produce their own creepy music beds. If you have the opportunity to do that, I strongly recommend it.

You may even find that you can generate revenue by selling some of your own music that you use in your haunt—the soundtrack to XYZ haunted house. I've never done that, but I've talked about it at great length. Since it's possible to purchase music on iTunes, Amazon, or whatever, it might be something to look into. I know more and more theme parks are starting to sell their audio from various and sundry attractions online, and you can download it. Disney has done this for years. People love it, because they want to relive that experience. You can pretty much do the same thing if you create your own creepy sounds for your haunted attraction.

Chapter 9

AUDITIONS—AND HOW TO SURVIVE THEM

In this chapter, I'm going to provide advice for how to make an unforgettable—in a good way—impression during an audition. Now, these tips aren't only applicable to auditions. I know some haunts don't even audition. They basically say, "You're tall, you'll fit the costume," and that's it. If that's the kind of haunt you're doing, these tips don't apply. However, more and more haunted attractions are doing some form of auditions for many different reasons, so the following are some recommendations based on my many years doing auditions for Howl-O-Scream in Tampa and for the last three seasons of The Vault of Souls as well as for other theatrical pieces that aren't necessarily Halloween-related.

I've seen a lot of people audition. I've seen a lot of people do some great and wonderful things, and I've seen a lot of people make some pretty silly and basic mistakes. I'm going to talk about how to audition without making some of the common mistakes that I've seen over the years. If you know someone who's not necessarily haunt-based but does auditions or is theater-based or interested in theater, this might be something to share with them. Maybe it will serve as a gateway drug so we can suck them into the dark side.

Auditions Get People Talking about Your Haunt Months Before Halloween

First of all, if you're a haunt owner, I think you should hold auditions. I realize it takes time and effort, but, if you hold auditions, that gives you a perfect reason to start talking about your haunt long before anybody really thinks about Halloween. A lot of the corporate haunts do their auditions early so they can get their costumes made and bring the right people on at the right time.

Auditions also get people talking about your event and, once you get your cast selected, *they* start chatting about it. Don't underestimate the power of social media. These folks are going to talk about how excited they are about being at XYZ haunt. It's just a really smart idea to start that buzz early.

Obviously, if you're holding auditions, you're going to get the best cast you can possibly find, and you can entice some folks you may not know. Plus, it keeps your cast fresh. Auditions are a perfect way to bring in some new blood and give you the opportunity to make sure everybody is on their A game.

Everything an Actor Does Is Part of the Audition

In this chapter, I'll focus on the actor's side rather than the owner's or director's side. Being a director, I'll probably slip back into that from time to time, but I'll try to stay focused as much as I can on what the haunt actor should think about.

Whether you're an actor auditioning for a haunted attraction, a theme park, a theatrical production, or whatever, be aware that every single thing you do is part of that audition. Every single time you make contact with whoever it is that's holding the audition, you're auditioning then and there. It's not just the two minutes when you're doing a monologue or when you're running back and forth in a room screaming in werewolf garb or whatever.

Auditions—and How to Survive Them

If you book your audition online, make sure you follow the directions for doing that. This was a really simple process for The Vault of Souls. I basically said, "Email your name and phone number to this email address, and you'll be assigned an audition time. No one will be seen without an audition time." That was in big, bold letters. I was shocked at how many people either didn't include their phone number or just showed up without an assigned audition slot. To me, that's a yellow flag, because I figure, if you can't follow directions in booking, how do I know you're going to follow directions if I hire you? Make sure you read those directions carefully and do exactly what you've been asked to do.

Always be polite. If you talk to somebody on the phone, be nice to them, because I'm not going to hire somebody I think is a jerk, no matter how talented they are. This aligns with the next tip: Be professional. Haunting is a ton of fun. In volunteer haunts and home haunts, things are often a bit looser, but the haunt industry is only going to continue to get better if everybody in it has respect for the industry itself and takes their "job" seriously. In my world, it's not only fun, it's fun we get paid to do, and it's fun that people pay to see. Therefore, we need to be professional at all times. So, book your audition time properly, and then show up.

Some organizations don't schedule audition times. They just say, "Show up between 9 and 2, and be prepared to audition." If auditions are running long, or running slowly, again, be professional. As we all know in the haunt industry, nothing—and I mean nothing—goes exactly as planned. If you demonstrate that you can patient and roll with it when things go awry, you'll already have a leg up on the folks who are complaining about how long something takes.

If You're Asked to Prepare, Prepare!

If you're asked to prepare something for the audition, make sure you *are* prepared. For The Vault of Souls, I asked people to do a two-minute, somber monologue. That's all I asked them to do. I told them, "You'll be cut off after two minutes. That doesn't mean I hate what I'm hearing. It means

I'm trying to keep us on schedule." I was pleased by how many people had prepared something. It was all over the board, and it was lovely, because it was so diverse. Some of the actor types went to a monologue book and found a creepy monologue. A couple people did selections from Edgar Allan Poe, which is always fine by me. I'm a big Poe fan, as those of you who know me have seen in some of the houses I've done in the past. I've got Edgar himself hanging on the wall of my office. Well, not himself. I have a lovely charcoal drawing of Edgar Allan Poe hanging on the wall of my office. He gazes at me, as does his raven and black cat. So, a few people did some Poe, but, unfortunately, they didn't memorize it. They read it, which is okay, except I never saw their eyes, and that's a little unfortunate in an audition.

Some people prepared but didn't prepare what they were asked to prepare. For example, I had a couple of people show up in costume, ready to go. Of course, The Vault of Souls had a very specific look. It was Tampa in the 1920s, and we didn't have any werewolves or vampires. We even had one person show up who had a full costume change—and it wasn't a quick change. I think it was supposed to be quick, but there were some costume malfunctions. Don't panic—we didn't see any body parts we weren't supposed to see. We had somebody show up in full character and never broke character throughout the entire audition process, which is fine, but again, that's not what was asked. Somebody came in and sang their audition, which was quite good, but again, not what was asked. These are red flags for me, because if you're not able to follow the directions of, "Come in and do this," how do I know I can trust you with guests for hours on end in a haunted attraction?

So, prepare what's asked, and prepare well. If you have a way to throw in a twist or something, that's great, but don't lead with the twist or gimmick. Lead with your talent. That's what I want to see, because, quite honestly, no matter what character I'm casting for, I'm probably going to costume you anyway. If you come in a costume, you're really hurting yourself. If someone comes in dressed as Count Dracula, they've shut themselves out, because I can't see them as anything other than a vampire. It works to your disadvantage to show up in a specific costume, because it limits the way people see you.

Show Up on Time

Showing up on time doesn't only mean not being late. I know how enthusiastic haunters can be, so don't show up two hours early. You're not queuing up for concert tickets in 1994. You don't have to wait in line or camp out. Show up 15 to 20 minutes before your scheduled time, if there's a schedule, because there will be paperwork or some organizational thing that needs to be done for the audition. Being there 15 minutes early is great, because then everything continues to run smoothly. One late person can back up the whole audition process. A casting director once told me, "On-time is late, so be there early." And, keep in mind, once you show up, your audition has already started. If you have to ask anybody for directions about how to get someplace or somebody asks you to park your car in a different location or whatever, your audition starts then. As I said, a lot of people won't hire jerks, so don't be one.

I've actually been in an audition where the person behind the desk who was signing people in walked into the audition room, pointed to a particular actor, and said, "That person was rude to me and isn't paying attention to what we're asking." That was great feedback, because that person auditioned quite well, but, if they were going to be difficult to work with, it wasn't worth it.

We're getting to the point now, especially in the haunt industry, where there are gobs and gobs of people out there who want work, so I won't hire somebody who's going to be a pain. Chances are good, too, they won't stick with me the entire season. It's much harder to jump onto a moving train, and it's much harder to recast mid-season. I want to get people in the first round that are good-to-great performers, are great-to-stellar people, and give them the tools they need and get out of their own way.

So, make sure you don't shoot yourself in the foot by arguing with the security guard outside the building where the auditions are being held. That's not in your best interest. Again, it goes back to being polite and being professional.

Advice for Haunt Owners and Casting Directors

Now I'm going to talk to the owners and casting directors for a moment. I've had owners say to me, "I'd love to have auditions, but I don't know what to have people do. My haunt is predominantly a series of startle scares, boo scares, drop doors, noisemakers, and that sort of thing. What should I have people do?" My response is to have them do drop doors, jump out, and say "Boo!" and "Rarrgh!" Have people audition by doing. That's the best way to see what your folks are capable of—and, believe it or not, it tests stamina. Anybody reading this knows how exhausting a haunted attraction can be—not just for the guests but for those of us performing in it. It's hard work. You wake up the next morning hurting in places you didn't know you had places. You want to test people's stamina and make sure they can do the gig. I've done auditions where it's all improvised, where people didn't have to prepare anything. I've done auditions where it's all prepared, and then I have them improvise on their prepared piece a little bit, just to see how well they follow direction. Either way, you have to look at the attraction you're doing and decide how you're going to audition based on that.

I was in auditions for 15 years at Howl-O-Scream, so I have bunch of funny and unusual stories, and I'll share a few. If you recognize yourself, don't feel bad. All these people were trying, so kudos to them. Some of them even got jobs—so, even better.

As I've mentioned, when you're in an audition, you have to make certain that you listen to the instructions. If you don't follow instructions at the audition, there's a good chance you won't follow direction and instructions at the actual event. This doesn't mean you can't embellish, show your best, and go over the top a little bit. That's great, that's wonderful. It's easier for a director to pull you back than push you forward. However, don't do things that aren't asked for. Don't do things that show you're out of control.

Let me give you an example. We were doing auditions, and I had an assistant say to this group of people, "When I walk by you, I want you to jump up, scare me, and sit back down." I was behind the audition table, and this person was running the audition. One actor jumped up, pulled out a butterfly knife, flipped it open, threatened us all with it, and then flipped it closed and put it back into his pocket. Yes, it was scary, but for all the wrong reasons. It was scary because it was out of control. That's just not appropriate. So, that's when we started adding various and sundry rules and regulations prior to the audition process such as: "Don't use any props. Don't do anything that could harm yourself or anyone around you." We had to add those things, because people get so excited and want to do something that puts them over the top. That was over the top, all right, but too far over the top. It overflowed and spilled down the sides, and that's not the way to get the job.

Another actor in that same audition was given the same direction, and he thought it would be really cool to kick his leg over the auditioner's head. The person who was running the auditions wasn't particularly tall, but this actor wasn't a particularly high kicker. He kicked the auditioner squarely in the back of the head. He was mortified and kept saying, "I'm so sorry, I'm so sorry." Again, this is another example of being out of control. As we all know, in any haunted attraction, safety is job one. If you break a safety rule or a basic safety concept in your audition, the director or the owner is going to think, "This person is likely to hurt somebody. We don't want that liability."

Everybody Wants You to Have a Great Audition

So, this brings us back to tips for actors. Listen *carefully* to the direction. At one audition, we had people running from one end of the room to the other as different characters. One of the characters we came up with was a rabid dog. I was looking for people who could be animalistic and physical, and I wanted to push them physically to see how they'd do. We had one performer who apparently misheard what was asked, and she had her hands up in front of her chest with her fingers pointing down and was hopping. Apparently, she heard "rabbit" dog not "rabid" dog. Or maybe she just heard "rabbit." Those are the moments when you're sitting behind the table and trying really hard not to laugh. You just have to look at them and think, "Bless your heart, you're trying. You really are trying. You're not doing well, but you really are trying." Listen to what you're asked to do. If you don't understand, it's okay to raise your hand and say, "I'm sorry, could you clarify what you want?" Anybody running auditions would be happy to do that.

What a lot of people who audition don't realize is, everybody sitting behind the audition table or wherever they happen to be and anybody watching the auditions wants you to do well. We don't want to see people fail. We don't want to see people who just aren't very good. We want everybody to be perfect. That makes our jobs easier on the one hand and harder on the other. Instead of realizing, "Oh my gosh, we don't have anybody," it's, "Oh my gosh, we have too many good people." It's a much better situation to be in when you have too many people who are excellent than not enough.

Remember this point when you go into an audition and you're feeling those nerves: The people watching you want you to be good, because it makes their job so much simpler. Show them how good you are, because, if you truly listen to the instructions, chances are your audition will be much better than if you go in there zoned out and don't pay attention.

The Audition Isn't Over When It's Over

When the audition is over, you're not done. When the audition is over, make sure you thank the audition team. I know this may seem like a silly thing, because it seems so formatted. However, if you're able to shake hands with the person doing the casting—or, at the very least, make eye contact with them—and say, "Thank you very much for your time," you're going to be remembered longer, and that's what you're trying to do at an audition—be remembered in a positive light.

I was at one group audition, a theatrical audition, and one kid finished his monologue—which was okay but somewhat forgettable—and then he said, "You'll remember me, because I'm the guy who showed you my nipples." He then lifted his shirt up over his head, showed us his nipples, and put his shirt down. Clearly, he accomplished part of his goal, because I'm still talking about it, and this happened probably 10 years ago. So, yes, I remember him, but I remember him as the idiot who didn't trust his own talent. He clearly didn't believe his monologue was going to be strong enough for us to remember him, so he had to do something silly, and it worked to his disadvantage.

However, I've had people who've come up to me, looked me in the eye, and said, "Thank you. I've wanted to work with you for a long time." Flattery will get you everywhere, but the fact that they made eye contact and said something to me makes me remember them in a far more positive light than, "I'm the kid who showed you my nipples." Dumb, dumb choice.

Don't Stay in Character after the Audition Is Over, and Forget the Gimmicks

When the audition is over, drop the character. If you stay in character the whole time, I haven't met you. I've met a character I didn't cast you in, and that makes me uncomfortable. I very much doubt I'd cast somebody who did this. At one audition, a woman came in who had had little acting ability, but she was an interesting character type. She'd worn a corset or cincher around her waist for many, many years and had something like a 14- or 15-inch waist, but her shoulders and hips were pretty much normal size. She walked in with a jacket draped over her shoulders, stood in the middle of the room, cast her eyes downward, and the person who'd walked in with her took the jacket off her shoulders to reveal this extreme hourglass figure. However, she wasn't able to do anything we asked her to do. It was all about this character she'd created. I'm sure there are opportunities for that, but they're few and far between.

As you can probably tell, I'm not a big proponent of gimmicky auditions. I'd much rather see you be well rehearsed, well prepared, clever, and committed. I'm not going to rely on a gimmick where you turn your back, put a mask on, and turn around wearing a mask. That's nothing I can work with. It may mean you're a great trick-or-treater, but you're not necessarily a good haunter.

Follow Up in a Professional Way

When you get home after the audition, send the audition team a quick email that says, "Thank you for seeing me." That sounds like sucking up, I know. The truth of the matter is, if you do that, once again, you're reminding that person of who you are in professional way. Don't say anything like, "Oh, I hope my audition was really good," or "If there's anything you think I can do, I really, really, really, really, really, really, really want to be cast." That's not good. Just thank them and say you hope to hear from them. For me, as the director, that reminds me, "Oh, right, there's that person." I may go back and look at their picture again, or I may go back and look at my notes for that person just because they contacted me. Again, you're showing that you're polite and professional.

After the casting is completed and everybody knows who made it—and, more importantly, who didn't—remember to be a gracious winner and a gracious loser. I hate using the word "loser," because casting isn't about winning or losing. Casting is about putting the right people in the right roles. In most of the haunted attractions I've done, I've rarely created characters based on who I saw in auditions. I'll have characters in mind that I've already written, and I'm looking for people who can fill certain roles.

In the majority of cases, not being cast doesn't mean you weren't good. It doesn't mean they don't like you. This is in my experience.

By the way, if you get mad for not being cast and rail about it on social media, keep in mind that people doing the auditions are probably looking at it as well. Other people who work in the haunt industry may also be looking at your social media page and thinking, "This person just ripped their potential employer to pieces, so I don't want to hire them."

So, those are my tips about auditions. Next, we're going to talk about the key to a great haunt—the actors—and how haunt directors can discover the right actors for the right roles and bring out the best in them.

Chapter 10

ACTORS REQUIRE CARE AND FEEDING

Actors make or break your haunt experience, so you need to take care of them. They're the lifeblood of any haunted attraction, so, in this chapter, we're going to talk about their care and feeding. That might sound condescending, but it's not. My background is in acting. I have a theater degree from Northern Illinois University with an emphasis on acting and directing. Actors are the lifeblood of any haunted attraction. You can have the coolest sets, the coolest lighting, the coolest special effects, and the coolest animatronics, but, if you have lackluster actors or not enough actors, your haunted attraction is going to be lifeless.

I'm going to share with you my views, what I've seen work, and things I've thought about trying but never have. First, I want to share a quote from screenwriter and film director Todd Solondz, who directed one of my favorite movies, *The Doll House*, and did work on *Dark Horse*, which I think he also wrote and directed. He says, "Casting is everything. If you get the right people, they make you look good." If you're a haunt owner and you have a crappy cast, you can yell at them as much as you want, but the fact is, they reflect you. You need to make every effort to make them good, because, if they screw up, the only person to blame is you. You didn't cast the right people, you didn't give them clear enough instruction, or you didn't keep a good enough eye on them. I'm not saying this to be hard on haunt owners. I say it to myself, too. If the actors in my haunt flop, it's my fault, so, I try to find the best people I possibly can.

Know What You're Looking For

Before you start auditioning haunt actors, it's important to know what it is you're looking for. As far as I'm concerned, there are basically two kinds of actors. One of them is what I call a character actor. These are people who can sustain characters for long periods of time and basically live as the character throughout the course of the night. The other kind of actor is what I call startlers. These are the folks who can scream like a crazy person all night long and not lose their voice. You have to understand the story you're telling to figure out how many of each of these two kinds of actors you need. I think most haunts need both kinds—if nothing else, you need some great queue actors. Once guests are inside, you can just do startles, which is fine. There's nothing wrong with that at all. I've seen that done very, very well.

You also have to figure out how much exposition and backstory you have to communicate. If you've got a lot of that to do, you're going to need more character actors and fewer startlers. Let me clarify—a character actor can do a startle as well, so you have to decide how many of those you need. On your cast list, you can make a notation—S for Startler, and C for Character. This helps you during the casting process to figure out how many of which you're looking for.

Before you start casting, you also have to take into consideration whether you're looking for stamina or style. Now, of course, you're going to say, "I want both." Well, that means you're going to have a huge challenge in casting, because stamina is something really seasoned pros have, and they'll still have style while they're doing it. Other folks get tired and unfocused. I'm sure none of you have ever walked around a corner of your haunt and seen one of your actors on their cell phone. There's nothing worse than seeing a werewolf on a cell phone. It just kinda blows everything out of the water, doesn't it?

Consider Double Casting

As the haunt owner and perhaps casting person, you'll have to decide if you want to give actors breaks or have them go full-tilt boogie for four to eight hours a night. If so, hire 14-year-olds and have lots of sugar and Coke backstage—I mean the soda. Or you might want to consider double casting. If you're able to make it so the performers have 30 minutes on and 30 minutes off, and you double cast, you can keep everything running smoothly nonstop. This is tough to do if you're already having trouble finding people, but, if you can do it, you'll have the freshest actors out there all the time, and you can expect more from them.

Another option is to have a full cast with breaks and include swings, which are actors who can go through and do break schedules. For example, Swing A covers the first five positions, rotates through them, and then takes a break. In The Vault of Souls, we had actors that were in the same rooms as five different characters, and that worked really well.

Be prepared for people who'll lose their voices, get tired, or won't make it back for the third weekend because they find haunt acting is a lot harder than they thought it would be. Take these things into consideration when you're casting, because you may discover you need 40 actors rather than 20. You want them to be high-energy, absolutely brilliant in every single moment, and make it through the full run, so you're going to have to double cast. If you open the last week of September, as many haunts do, everyone is super high-energy and excited the first weekend. The guests are pounding down the door, because it's the beginning of the haunt season. Then, you go through the doldrums, which is usually the second and third weekend until you get to the second weekend in October, when it starts to ramp up again. By the time you get to the weekend before Halloween, in many cases, you'll have lost a significant number of your cast. If you haven't, congratulations. That means you're doing everything absolutely right. We're going to talk a little bit later about how to retain actors.

So, decide up front if you want to double cast, what break schedule you want, and what you're looking for, and find a balance in all of that.

Every Performer Needs Compensation, but that Doesn't Have to Be Money

Every performer needs to be compensated in some way. Now, when I say compensation, that doesn't necessarily mean money. If you can pay your actors, great. If you can say, "We'll give you 2% of the profit," do that. I haven't talked to many haunts that have tried profit sharing, and I think the reason is, when most haunts first start out, the first part of that phrase doesn't exist. They're more than willing to share, but there's not a lot of profit. If you can profit share, that means you're paying with money you've already made. I like to say we're paying actors with the guests' money, not your money. It also encourages your actors to market for you, to promote your haunt. The more people they can get to come to the haunt, the more money they'll end up making in the long run.

You can also pay people in experience, especially if you're a volunteer haunt. You can give them acting training classes and makeup training classes. I know one place that does this instead of paying actors for rehearsals. They say, "After you take this haunt-acting class (which is essentially the rehearsal process), we'll give you this makeup training class, and you have to take this safety training class. After you've completed all those, we'll start paying when the event opens."

Another way to keep your actors coming back is to make sure they always have cold water and some sort of snack. If you build the right dynamic into your cast, your cast will bring in food as well. Some break rooms look like a buffet or family picnic. You can reinforce actors' participation by letting them know there will be pizza every night. You might be able to get those pizzas donated if you're a volunteer haunt or a haunt trying to raise money for a good cause. You might be able to go to your local pizza restaurant and say, "If you provide us with pizzas every night for our cast, we'll put your name on our tickets." Feeding your actors is definitely a form of compensation.

Another great compensation is recognition. This is something I like to do wherever I can. In one haunt, I had buttons printed up that said, "I

Scared Scott." If I went through the haunted attraction and saw an actor going above and beyond, they'd get one of these buttons. The second year, we added what we called Gold Coins, which were redeemable for some amount of cash, and these were used as rewards as well. I discovered that the majority of performers would rather have the button that said "I Scared Scott" than the coin that was good for $10 cash. Each button cost me 22 cents or something like that.

Haunt actors are an odd and wonderful group of people, and they love to be recognized when they do a good job. If they wanted to make tons and tons of money doing anything else, they'd probably be doing it. Haunt acting is the hardest job you'll ever miss when it's over. You'll sweat like you've never sweated before, you'll hurt everywhere, and you'll want to come back the next night. Giving recognition for that kind of commitment is indeed a form of compensation.

Don't Ignore the Small Print

A most important thing to look at before you start casting are your local labor laws. How long are you going to be open? Are you going to be open during the week? I'm not here to give you legal advice except that you should look into the laws. Make sure you can hire people under the age of 18 if they're working X number of hours and you're able to give them zero breaks. If you hire children, do you need to have a parent there, and how often do you need to give them breaks? Do they need to have a separate break room? I realize some of you are thinking, "I don't even want to deal with that." My recommendation is don't hire kids and don't hire folks you're going to have to make special arrangements for, because it's just going to make for bigger headaches than you need. Of course, I'm always pushing for every haunt—whether it's a home haunt or a high-end private haunt or a theme-park haunt—to run at a professional, safe level. Be creative so you don't need to cast people who are underage.

"Where Can I Find Haunt Actors, and How Can They Find Me?"

Now that we've talked about knowing what kind of actors you need and how many, the next question is, where can haunt owners find actors? Conversely, where can haunt actors find haunt owners? If you're a haunt owner, don't think for a minute there aren't people out there who want to be in your haunt. And, if you're a haunt actor, don't think haunt owners don't want to see you because you don't have a lot of experience. You guys are both looking for each other. You just have to find ways to make that connection. If both sides make an effort, it will make casting much, much simpler.

The first thing I suggest is considering the people who've worked for you before. If your cast the previous year did a great job, get as many of them back as you can the following year. Treat your cast like your after-dark family. Make them feel they have a sense of ownership in what they're doing. Create an experience for them that they want to come back to.

The best way to retain people is to treat them well. What this means is, if you're the person in charge, or if you're the person who trained or hired them, make an appearance when they're working. Don't give them notes without watching them. Give them the validation that what they do is important enough to get some of your most important commodity—your time. If you do that, you'll not only retain your cast, you'll also get a great returning cast for the following year. Stay in touch with that wonderful cast. Create a Facebook group where you can keep tabs on everybody throughout the course of the year—who's doing what, who's able to come back, who's not able to come back. That's a huge benefit.

One of the things you can do with a returning cast is a recommendation program. This means the person who recommends the greatest number of new people who are hired gets a $50 bonus. That's $50 you don't have to spend in advertising your auditions, and, in the grand scheme of things, it's nothing. This is probably the best targeted advertising for your auditions. The people who know what the job is will go to their friends—who they want to work with—and try to convince them to come and work for you. That's worth way more than $50.

Social media is certainly a way to reach a lot of people. Now, this doesn't happen overnight. It isn't posting once, and you're done. By the same token, this is something that absolutely every haunted attraction can and should do—not just for the guest-facing elements but for the cast, too. Everybody reading this could start a Facebook group right now of the cast of your haunted attraction. You could make it a private group, so only people who are cast members can join, and all you need to do is hang onto that. Again, keep that contact year-round.

Many cities have Facebook pages and Facebook groups for casting. Go into Facebook, put in the search words "auditions" or "casting" and the name of your city. You'll find Facebook pages and Facebook groups that gather the people you're looking for. You can join those groups and start posting in those groups. Also, look at convention pages on social media—Transworld, HAuNTcon, Midwest Haunters, Chicago Frights, Spooky Empire, West Coast Haunters, Mid-Summer Scream, and all the others I can't remember right now—and see who's part of those Facebook pages, if they're public, and throw a little note out there—"We're looking for haunt actors." You'll be surprised how many people will travel to audition for your haunt.

You also might want to look not just at haunt actors but at people in similar kinds of events that haunters enjoy. Look for cosplayers, because, quite often, cosplayers will "slum" in haunted attractions. Also check out Renaissance Faires. If you can get in with the RenRats, you'll find more haunters than you know what to do with. Then, obviously, there are community theaters and professional theaters.

You're Not Necessarily Looking for "Actors"

I've heard a lot of people say, "I don't like to hire 'actors,' because they're difficult to work with." My response to that is, "You're not hiring good actors. You're hiring mid-range actors who can't get work anywhere else, so they think they're a lot more important than they are." I say this as an actor. I'm not out to slam anyone individually, but there are a group of folks who think their poop don't smell, and they're wrong. This means that you, as a director or haunt owner, have to treat those 'actors' a little bit differently. You have to communicate differently.

What you're really looking for are people who love Halloween and aren't afraid to look silly. If you think you're super cool, you're not going to be a good haunt actor. You need to be able to throw on some makeup and put on a really bad wig and some fangs. A lot of folks don't want to walk down the street looking like that, and a lot of haunt actors do walk down the street looking like that. I don't discount using actors just because some haunt folks don't feel it's easy to work with actors. You just have to understand them and hire the right ones—which are the actors willing to work with you. If they think they're above you, don't hire them. It's that simple.

Also, check your local schools. There are theater departments in almost every college and community college. If there's no theater department, check with the English department, the communications department, or mass communications, and you might find some folks interested in acting in your haunt. Check with fraternities and sororities. If you're a low-budget or volunteer haunt, get in touch with a fraternity or sorority and say, "If you're able to provide us with 10 people who want to act in our haunt and who go through all of our training, we'll make a donation to your fraternity or sorority of $200." Again, this is significantly cheaper than paying your individual performers, and you're still considered a volunteer haunt. You're also developing a relationship with an organization that will not only be able to provide you with actors but also with patrons. If you get 10 fraternity brothers to come in and be part of the haunt, you'll get significantly more fraternities and sororities that will support the haunt and pay money to watch their friends be monsters or demons.

So, those are just a few of the suggestions for where to find actors.

Why Auditions Are Essential

Next is the audition, which we talked about at length in the previous chapter. We used to call this "casting," because some people are afraid of the word "audition." My feeling is, if they're afraid to "audition," they're probably afraid to perform in your haunt. So, go ahead and use the word audition. As I said previously, I'm adamant about auditions, because they help you avoid bad casting. You don't want to just put people who are interested in working for you in costumes without knowing anything about them. That's bad casting. Auditioning also gives value to the performers. If they have to audition, and they have the experience of being selected, there's that wonderful endorphin rush of, "I got cast!" They'll be very excited about that and, hopefully, they'll post about it on their Facebook page, which is another way to advertise your auditions and starts people talking about your haunt. I recommend doing auditions sometime in July—maybe June, maybe August—but over the summer in any case. This gives you the opportunity to talk about your haunted attraction way before the season begins. It also means you can get people who can commit to the time you need them to commit to

Make the auditions fun. More important than the content is the attitude surrounding the audition. Make it a Halloween party over the summer. That way, you attract the people interested in Halloween. Clearly state, up front, that you're doing auditions, but invite people to bring their friends, serve snacks if you want to, have swag or giveaway so people get something for coming to the audition. This makes them feel better, and it encourages them talk up the audition later.

Audition by Doing

When you actually get into the audition itself, don't have people come in, say their names, and tell you they want to be a werewolf or whatever. You have no idea whether they can be a werewolf. They have to audition by doing. Also, the audition brings up any challenges they may have with the job. If you've never been a haunt actor, you don't know how hard it is. It's harder than most people can imagine.

Having people audition by doing allows you to see whether they can hack it. Do they need to come in with prepared material, like a monologue, a story, or a joke? No, they don't. Much better is to have a series of improvised games for them to do, and I'll give you some examples shortly. See how they think on their feet, so to speak. That's far more impactful than a prepared monologue—unless you're doing a haunt that's predominantly atmospheric, in which case you need a bunch of actory actors.

If somebody has the right energy and the passion, you can tell that right off the bat when you're watching them audition. If you somebody is good and has the right look, give them something to read or have them improvise something in front of you. For example, you can say, "I'd like you to cast an evil spell or a curse over everybody at the audition table," and see what they do. If they come up with something that makes you feel uncomfortable and creepy, you should probably hire them.

The Four Things to Look for in an Audition

So, what do you look for when you're watching people do their auditions? My criteria are really pretty simple. There are four things I look for in an audition. The first is their character development. Do they develop a character during the course of the exercise they've been given? Are they living in that character, or are they looking at the people next to them to see what they're doing? I have a tendency to audition in groups, usually groups of 10, because I want to see how the actors work together as a team. Are they developing characters that work to enhance what the other people are bringing to the table, or are they trying to showboat and steal attention?

The audience connection is huge. Again, a haunted attraction isn't like standard theater. There isn't what's called the fourth wall. Actors can see the audience. In fact, the audience is the missing character during the rehearsal process. The audience plays a character, so make certain the actors connect with whoever is watching them and with each other.

Are they able to startle and reset? For many years at Howl-O-Scream, we had to put a ton of guests through the houses every single night. We needed to make certain that everybody working there could scare and reset, scare and reset, scare and reset so every single guest got every single scare. Were we 100% successful? No, but I think we did better than most. It's important to know if an actor has the ability to startle and reset—not startle and linger until somebody wants to punch them.

Finally, there's the issue of stamina, which I mentioned a few pages ago. If an actor is having trouble catching their breath by the end of your audition, chances are good they ain't gonna hang for a whole night, and they'll probably leave after the first weekend. So, make sure you look at those four things—character development, connection with the other people in the room—including the audience, startle and reset, and stamina.

Games to Use at Auditions

What kind of games can you use to audition people? I call them games because, like I said, the audition should be fun. I start out my group of 10 with instructions about safety—they can't do anything that will knowingly harm themselves or anyone around them, they can't use any props to scare me, and they can't touch anyone in the room. After that, I put them through some sort of physical activity. I'll find an excuse for them to run or move back and forth from one side of the room to the other. As they're doing that, I'll have them change characters. For example, they're in a creepy library and they're picking up books from one side of the room, stacking them on a shelf on the other side of the room, going back to get books on the first side of the room, and they continue going back and forth. Or, they're digging a grave on one side of the room and dumping the dirt on the other side. You can come up with any idea or plot device you want. As they do this, I call out different characters and see how quickly they adapt to those characters. I see if there are changes in the way they walk, their posture, the sounds they make. Hopefully, a transforming werewolf sounds different than an 18th-century vampire who sounds different than a victim being chased in the dark. My hope is they'll be able to identify all three of those characters and play them clearly.

After they do that, I like to do something to test their ability to startle and reset. If you have the opportunity to have drop doors set up or have some of the scare locations from your house, you can take small groups to a single room in your haunt and tell each person to find a location. Then you say, "I'm going to walk through the room, and I want you to scare me." This is very practical. It's scaring by doing. Walk through a few of times, because somebody may miss their opportunity the first time. If they miss it the second or third time, you might not want to hire them.

If I see somebody special, I'll ask them to come out and do something as an individual. That doesn't happy too often, because I know who the people are in my locale. However, every now and then I'll get somebody and think, "Where did they come from? They're really good. Let's hire them."

So, that's basically an audition that will work for pretty much anybody. You have it all written down here, so you can refer to it any time.

Training Your Actors

Once you've got your actors cast, the issue is training them. Training is another form of compensation. Make sure you have people who know how to train them to do really good makeup. Your actors can assist with the costume construction—or, even more fun, the costume destruction. Get costume pieces and let them be part of the team that adds the dirt, the blood stains, the Great Stuff that looks like intestines flowing out. Give them that training, because it also gives them a great deal of ownership.

The most important thing, when it comes to training, is safety. It's the thing nobody wants to make fun, but you need to, because it has to sink in. You need to find that balance between fun and serious, because safety is job one in any haunt, always. You have to reinforce that and drive it home. At the very least, with your safety training, have an evacuation plan and execute it. When you sound this buzzer, when this light goes off, when the audio goes out in the haunt, when all the house lights come on, practice what an evacuation looks like. Don't just tell them, "Go out this door." Say, "During tonight's rehearsal, we're going to do a practice evacuation," and make sure you get everybody out.

It's important to teach your actors how to do some sort of physical warm-up before going out and doing their job—stretching, calisthenics, whatever. Have them do some sort of cardio to get their heart rate up. Equally important is vocal warm-up, because we all know what actors' voices sound like the day after opening. So, do some sort of vocal warm-up, do some sort of physical warm-up, and practice an evacuation plan. Also, make sure everyone knows where the fire extinguishers are. That's very, very important. Safety can destroy everything you've tried so hard to do if you don't do it right. So, make sure that works.

I'm just giving you the bare minimum here about haunt-actor training. The Haunted Attraction Association has significantly better and more in-depth training, and you should definitely look into that.

During rehearsal, make sure you identify to your performers which of them are atmosphere and which of them are startle. Sometimes you have be as blatant as telling each one, "You're here to create an atmosphere," or "You're here to create a distraction." You can be more specific, like, "Don't scream, just follow people in the queue. Reach out like you're going to touch their hair or get really close to their ear and make them uncomfortable." With startles, make sure you have them practice startling and resetting. My rule of thumb is that every fifth person in a conga-line-style haunted house should be startled. So, it's like, "BLAH!" two, three, four, five, "BLAH!" You can count that rhythm out if you want to.

Make sure your actors understand the story of the house—the beginning, middle, and end—and how they fit into that story. They need to know what happens before them and what happens after them. If they know the distraction or scare from the previous room and what's coming up next, they can distract guests from that. Haunting is truly a team sport, so they have to know how they fit into the grand scheme of things. If you're a haunt owner, a trainer, or an acting coach, you need to know that better than they do, so you can help them find it.

Teach Your Actors to Read Guests

Work with your actors to help them figure out how to read guests, and train them to do this. If you scare certain folks, they'll hurt you, and my recommendation is, don't poke that bear. If you scare other folks, it will make the rest of the group laugh. The guy that's so nervous he's holding his girlfriend in front of him and trying to give the impression she's the scared one—if you can scare him, the whole group has that sense of instant karma immediately, and that's a lot of fun.

Also, train your actors to identify which guests have had a little bit too much to drink or their personality has been altered by some other chemical. Oh, and kids. Invariably, no matter what you tell people about the recommended age group for your haunt, some people will bring a three-year-old that gets terrified. Some three-year-olds will think it's all very funny, but others will be absolutely mortified. We're out to entertain, not to traumatize. If you can give that child the power to scare *you*, you'll provide them with a whole new level of confidence. So, make sure your performers understand that different guests need to be handled in different ways.

Retain Your Actors by Catching Them Doing Things Right

We've got the actors cast, we've got them trained, and now we go into maintaining their performance. I truly believe that any performance experience needs to end as strong or stronger than it started, and that's tough. Most haunted attractions run at least 10 nights, and some run 50 nights. Maintaining the performance throughout that time is really, really challenging. The biggest tool you have is observation. If you're an owner and you can pull yourself away to walk through your haunted attraction at least three times a night—not always at the same time—that's the best way to learn what's going on. You can see how your actors are doing at scaring—not at scaring you but scaring the people in front of you and the people behind you. Catch them doing things right. If you catch things being done right, you'll train people to do things right. If you go through and make 20 notes on your actors, at least 10 of them need to be, "That was great!" The other 10 can be things like, "You were too slow on your reset," or, "What the hell happened to your makeup? Why are you a clown? That doesn't fit." If you catch them doing things wrong, tell them why they're wrong, in private, and then offer them an alternative—"The way you did it isn't right, but maybe you can try this instead."

As I mentioned before, it's important to reward good behavior publicly and redirect privately to maintain the quality of performance throughout the entire run. Share the 10 "That was great!" notes in front of the cast. If you need to redirect somebody, find a casual way to talk to that person privately. This builds morale and doesn't embarrass your cast. I've had cast members who did something really stupid, and then I did something really stupid by making a big deal out of it in front of the rest of the cast. Those actors were so embarrassed they didn't come back the next night.

Praise can take the form of swag or other materials you use to promote the event, like the "I Scared Scott" buttons I mentioned earlier. There's a company online called One Inch Round that sells one-inch round pins—and other sizes as well—in large quantities for very little money per pin. That's a great way to provide actors with a brag tag of, "I did good!"

Don't forget to maintain your expectations to the end. As I said at the beginning of this chapter, if you're actors are great, it reflects well on you. If your actors aren't great, it reflects poorly on you. You need to maintain your expectations all the way through the run. If you're able to do that, you'll be able to clearly communicate to your cast what's good, what's not, what you like, and what you don't like. For years, I've used the mantra—"Start, stop, continue." Train your cast to start doing things they're not doing that they should be, stop doing things they shouldn't be, and continue doing things that are right. If you train them in this way from the beginning, that "continue" category will be the biggest.

Chapter 11

Make It Good, Make It Fast, or Make It Cheap—Pick Two

In the final chapter of this section on operations, I'm going to give you tips and tricks for using your creativity to have the most awesome haunt ever... and save money. I'm a firm believer you don't need a huge amount of finance to make a really cool haunted experience. When I say that, people often reply, "Yes, Scott, but you've worked for Busch Gardens and The Vault, you've always had big budgets," and blah, blah, blah. That's true, I have, but you'd be surprised how, even with big-budget events, some of the coolest things come from those cheap little creative ideas. Part of the reason we could do so much at Busch Gardens Howl-O-Scream, The Vault of Souls, or any of the haunt projects I've worked on is because we were frugal. We tried to find creative ways to make things happen.

I should probably start by saying that one of my favorite phrases is, "Make it good, make it fast, or make it cheap—pick two." You can make it good and fast, but it ain't gonna be cheap. You can make it good and cheap, but it ain't gonna be fast. You can make it cheap and fast, but it ain't gonna be good. What we're going to focus on is finding ideas and ways to make things cheap and good, because, let's face it, we all have to think about money, whether you're a professional haunter—where making money is a big factor—or a home haunter who wants to get as much as you can for your dollar. If you can do a full, front-yard haunt for $50, and it looks like a million bucks, that's what you want to do. If you're a professional haunter who's focusing on getting the most out of your investment, you obviously want to spend as little as you possibly can and still have a high-end, quality product.

The key is to use your creativity. Here's another phrase I use: "Creativity will provide." If you're creative, you'll find a way to make your budget work. That creativity may mean you have to slightly tweak or rewrite your storyline, or it may mean you have to think a little bit outside the box, or it may mean you have to call in favors from friends, or it may mean you have to build your own props.

Tricks Used in Famous Movies

Being cheap and still being good—sometimes even iconic—has been going on in film for years and years and years. I want to share with you a couple of my favorite stories. The movie *Monty Python and the Holy Grail* was made on a shoestring budget and went on to earn a fortune. In certain scenes, they're shooting up a hill, and there's a castle in the background. The castle is just a cardboard cutout painted to look like a castle. This is hard to see, and the only reason I know about this is because I looked it up. Of course, if it's on the Internet, it's got to be true. The scene with the iconic coconuts and the clop-clop was originally supposed to be a big sequence with real horses, but the horses got cut from the budget. So, they came up with something creative and clever, and it became iconic.

Another fun example from the horror-film genre is the Michael Meyers mask. A lot of you may know this, but I just recently found out about it, and it makes me laugh. The original Michael Meyers mask was a William Shatner-Captain Kirk mask that was painted white, so it didn't look like Shatner. Apparently, when they went to make some of the sequels to *Halloween,* they found only one of the original *Halloween* masks, because they weren't anticipating the first movie becoming a full franchise. They found markings on the neck of the mask that said, "Don Post," and there was a number. They contacted Don Post and read off the number. "That's our Captain Kirk mask," was the reply. So, it just shows you don't have to spend a bazillion dollars to have your own private mask made. Get something that already exists for a few bucks, paint it, and it can become iconic.

Here's another example of something that happened in a movie. In the original Star Trek movie—*Star Trek: The Motion Picture*—there's a space station that's actually a model. This is back in the day before they did everything with CGI. That exact same model is used again in *Star Trek Two: The Wrath of Khan,* but, in that movie, the model was repainted and flipped upside down. If you search online, you can see stills from both movies and see that, yup, it's the same model flipped upside down.

Creating Affordable Scenery— Reuse, Repaint, and Repurpose

That's a perfect example of our first topic, or part of our first topic, which is how to do affordable scenery for your haunts. Please don't do black Visqueen walls unless you truly think black Visqueen is exactly what the walls should be covered with. If you're doing a slaughterhouse or something, maybe you might be able to get away with black Visqueen, but I've seen so many people decide to slap up black Visqueen and say, "It's black, so it's got to be scary." No, it's black, and that means you can't see it. To me, it feels like being trapped in a giant garbage bag. I suppose there are ways to make it work, but you've got to be clever.

My initial advice, when it comes to scenic, is to reuse what you've got. One of the nice things about working at Busch Gardens back in the day was we had a full warehouse of stuff that came from earlier years of Howl-o-Scream and other shows. So, reuse stuff, and write based on what you have. If you have access to a bunch of chain-link fencing, write something that takes place in a junkyard—or even a tennis court. That might seem like a really bad idea, although you know my theory—come up with a story, add the phrase, "gone horribly, horribly wrong," and you've got a haunted attraction. The idea of reusing stuff is you can throw a coat of paint on something, and people won't be able to tell what it was before. Once you've got the walls of your haunt, you can reposition them and move them around. If you want to learn more about this, Leonard Pickel has probably some of the cleverest ways of making things modular. I'm clearly not smart enough in that area. So, reuse, repaint, and repurpose.

We did the same thing at Howl-o-Scream as was done with the model in the two Star Trek movies—but with full-size houses. We'd take a haunted house, turn it around, and make the entrance the exit and the exit the entrance. There was a house called Trapped in the Walls. For the first two years, we ran it from one direction, and then someone said, "From an operations standpoint, Scott, it would be much easier if we ran it the other way." Of course, as the creative guy, I dug in my heels and said, "No! It was designed to be done this way, and we can't do it the other way." They said, "Scott, please just walk it backwards." Sure enough, after I walked it backwards, we turned a few props around, changed a few rooms, and made an entirely new house just by changing the way guests experienced it. That's the ultimate in reusing what you've already got.

Another example from Howl-o-Scream involved a zombie containment unit or ZCU. All of the zombie containment unit, all of that haunted house, was pulled from the warehouse, because we had to make it fit within certain budget numbers. This is another case of writing based on what you have. Write based on what you can get your hands on cheaply and easily. If Visqueen happens to be it, write a haunt where you're using clear plastic tarps because everything takes place in a sterile environment, so it has to be wrapped in plastic. That gives it its own sort of style.

My cheap tip is to plan ahead and plan accordingly. If you have a bunch of junker cars, they make great set pieces. Sometimes you have to take the motors out and drain all the fluids, depending on whoever the fire marshal is in your area, but still, they're big, cheap props. Write something that uses those.

Use What's Already There

A variation on reusing is taking advantage of what's already there. Write to what's already in the space. I first learned this from John Hawkins and the guys at Oak Island when I was working at Howl-O-Scream years and years ago. We did a house called The Labyrinth of Lost Souls. There was a big power panel in the space where we were building the haunted house that wasn't used anymore. It was gigantic, really cool looking, and very, very expensive to get out of there. So, we incorporated it into the story and actually duplicated it later in the story. The whole concept of the house was being stuck in purgatory and coming back to the same room again. We never would have had that inspiration if we hadn't looked at what we already had, because we didn't have to pay a dime for that first big power panel—and, we saved money by using it, because we didn't have to tear it down and haul it away.

Probably the most glaring example—or the most wonderful example, depending on your perspective—of using what's already there was in The Vault of Souls. When I wrote The Vault of Souls, one of the star rooms for the three years we did it was the actual vault itself. I never ever could have afforded—on any budget—to build something that amazing. The door itself was 18 tons, it was very intricately done, and the vault was just a beautiful space. So, taking what you've got and working it into your storyline is a great way to save money.

Exchange Sweat Equity for Free Materials

If you've got local construction companies looking for help in tearing stuff down, take advantage of that. A member of my family was a rather clever carpenter, and he used to work with local construction companies to help them with renovations, because there's always some sort of a demolition phase. He'd say, "I'll come in and help you demo if I can have what I take down." He collected church pews, beautifully carved wooden doorframes, and all kinds of amazing stuff pretty much for free, because he put in the sweat equity.

You can do that on a much smaller scale. Find a local contractor in your area and say, "I'm looking for parts and pieces for my haunt." This can be hardware, doorknobs, hinges, all kinds of stuff. If you're careful, you can get some usable lumber. We've all done haunts that have toilets in them, so you could probably get free or very inexpensive toilets. If it's a general contractor, you can offer to put in the sweat equity to take some of the stuff you tear down. You haul it away to your garage, warehouse, or directly to your haunt if you keep the space year-round.

To sum up, write your story based on what you have available—whether it's the location or things you can tear out of other people's buildings or things you've used in other haunted houses that you can turn upside down and paint a different color. This will save you a ton of money and still make everything look new and fresh.

Great Sources for Costumes

People doing haunts often think, "Costuming will be easy. We'll just put people in hobo costumes and masks and call it a day." This is probably not the best approach. Many of you have heard me say it's important to have a costume designer. It's important to have somebody who can be the overarching eye to see how all the costumes come together, especially if you're doing anything in a particular period of history.

Instead of going out and buying all your costumes from a costume house, you're going to be better served buying clothes somewhere else. Pretty much all the costumes at Howl-O-Scream were old show costumes that we redid. The costume team would rebuild them, repurpose them, or distress them, but they were all reused stuff. Quite often we'd go to the warehouse, walk around, and write something to match the costuming we found.

If you don't have a full costume warehouse like Busch Gardens did or access to old costume storage, go to your local thrift stores. Do this not after you've decided what sort of haunt you're going to do but before you start writing. Walk up and down the aisles. There might be a ton of men's suits or really lame prom or bridesmaids' dresses from the 1980s. You can take a bunch of old bridesmaids' dresses, bloody them up, and do an entire zombie prom.

Reach out to your friends. Keep an eye on Facebook. You'd be surprised how many people are willing to give stuff away just to get it out of their house. Remember the costumes I got from that that cruise line that I mentioned earlier? Along with the costumes, I got a giant bolt of orange fur. I have no idea what I'm going to do with it—maybe create a giant muppet of some sort. I got some hats, some masks, and some old, tattered wigs. The cool thing about haunts is you can get the grungiest stuff, and you don't have to distress it yourself. All you need to do is clean it. If it doesn't look grungy enough, there are many, many inexpensive ways to grunge up costumes.

Fun with Great Stuff™, Sobo Fabric Glue, and Cheese Graters

First and foremost is the haunter's number-one tool, Great Stuff. You can create anything from dirt to brains to intestines depending on how you use it. Great Stuff doesn't wash out of fabrics—ever—so the clothes don't reek but remain nicely distressed.

If you're trying to create something that looks like vomit, mucus, pus, or anything like that, Sobo Fabric Glue is for you. Sobo Fabric Glue dries clear with a little bit of a sheen, and you can add color to it. If want to make it look like vomit, you can do that. I often like to put a layer of it over blood. Use acrylic paint, cover it with Sobo Glue, and it looks like wet blood, wet vomit, wet mucus, or wet whatever you want it to look like. After it dries, it stays in the fabric and looks really good.

The other thing I strongly recommend people invest in when they're making their own haunt costumes is junked-up cheese graters, wood rasps, or files, because you'll use these on fabric all the time to wear out knees, rip out pockets, shred, and whatever, so it doesn't look like that bad zig-zag cut that people do at the bottom of jeans to try to make them look like they're worn out. Don't do that. Take a cheese grater, bundle up the bottom of the jeans, and rub the fabric over the cheese grater until the fabric starts to shred. That way, it actually looks aged rather than cut by the mom of a fourth grader who got wrangled into doing the costumes for the school play.

I always say, "Dirty stuff up. Don't make it look new." If it looks like it just came out of a bag from Party City, there's something wrong. You've got to add your own touches to it and grunge it up. One time, I was an actor in a student film shot in the woods in Illinois where this eccentric person had built a small castle. The scene was supposed to be a medieval broad-sword fight with a demon. I was handed this clean, pressed costume, which didn't make any sense given the scene and my character. So, I found a mud puddle near my car, threw the costume into the mud puddle, ran my car back and forth over it a few times, got it all grungy, and ripped out the hems. So, use your cheese graters and your imagination.

Clever Ideas for Inexpensive Masks and Manikins

People often ask me if there's a cheap way to do masks. One idea is to take a latex mask, cut it apart, and reapply it to a nylon stocking. This gives you a completely moveable mask, similar to a silicon mask. I like taking burlap sacks or pillowcases and creating characters who feel they're so hideously deformed they need to cover their faces. You can get old pillowcases, put drawstrings in them, cut out eyes, put some sort of mesh behind the cutouts, and then make it look like blood is seeping through the pillowcase. People's imaginations make them think, "Oh, I'm glad he's wearing that pillowcase over his head. I don't really want to see what's under there." This is cheap and effective.

You can also get cheap, beat-up manikins. I've even known people who have used inflatable dolls—the kind that are normally used for more… private purposes. I've seen them take those, dress them, and use them as remarkably inexpensive manikins. Manikins are pricey, and if you're doing a traditional statue scare where there's manikin-manikin-actor-manikin-manikin-manikin, the manikins almost always look like manikins. I strongly recommend going to your thrift store, buying some jumpsuits—or just pants, shirts, and shoes—stitching them together, filling them with old newspapers, and putting a mask over where the head would be. That mask could be one of your pillowcases. If you've got five people lined up with pillowcases over their heads, and one of them comes to life, it will be effective and very inexpensive. If you can afford posable manikins, great, but this is for those folks who have the time and the interest. Stitch all the clothing together, stuff it with newspaper, and pose the manikins, which will make them look more like real people. Manikins are all built to a perfect size, so stuffed clothes look fat and bunchy. You may have to sit them in a chair and maybe glue them in place, so they look like they're sitting naturally. This is a cheap way to make manikins. If you put the same mask on the manikin that you put on the actor, your guests will never be able to tell the difference, and you'll scare the heck out of them.

Super Cheap Makeup Ideas

Let's move on to some super cheap makeup ideas. One of my absolute favorite cheap makeup ideas for haunted attractions is a mud mask. I've done this a few times, and I just used it again recently for a photo shoot. I was doing a sample photo, and I needed something to change the texture of my skin. I used a mud mask that has actual mud or clay in it. There are many that dry with a gel quality to them, which is cool for something different, but I wanted that pasty, rotting-away kinda look. I took that mud mask, put it all over my face and through my hair, and let it dry. Then I powdered it all white and drew really awful clown makeup on top of that. This is super cheap and super effective.

After the mask dries, when you move your face, the mask cracks. If you want, you can fill in those cracks to make them more obvious. They might look like age lines, or they might look like you're decomposing.

You can use this for clowns, mummies, and zombies. Mud masks come in different colors—gray, green, brown, and some that dry almost white. At the end of the night, you just wash it all off. It doesn't stick in your hair, and your face feels great. You've gotten a facial during the course of your day!

Another cool aspect of the mud mask is it sweats off during the course of the night. You can reapply it, or you can just let the chips fall off, and that creates another look. If it gets kind of gunky from sweating, when you take your break or sit in front of a fan, it dries again and looks just as wonderfully gross.

When it comes to makeup, don't skimp on brushes. Get yourself three or four really good makeup brushes and one or two really good makeup sponges. You can use crummy sponges at other times. There's an egg-shaped silicon sponge that's excellent for blending and applying color. If you know what you're doing with makeup, great, but, if you don't, having the right tools will really help you.

As far as brushes go, get a giant, fluffy, powder brush to apply powder at the end to set your makeup. My favorite brush is a two-sided brush. It has an angled tip on one side and a fine tip on the other. I like it because you can flip it around in your hand to do detail work, big block work, and blend it together with your little egg-shaped sponge. Get a contour brush, or blush brush, which is a shorter-bristled, fuller brush. With these basic brushes, you can pretty much do anything you want to. Of course, you want to take care of your brushes, clean them properly, and clean your silicone sponge properly. If you're using crap makeup sponges, you can just throw them away. However, getting better-quality tools can be less expensive in the long run.

If you can get a good deal on a professional makeup kit, do that, but you can basically go to any drug store, Target, Walmart, or whatever and get regular foundation makeup. If you get a really pale color—a white or super light beige—a black, a brown, and a red, you can do some pretty incredible things, especially if you're doing it over something like a mud mask, which already has all that texture. All you have to do is use your color to add a little oomph.

For haunt purposes, the best lipstick is usually the cheapest. For some reason, it stays on better, and it stains better. There's a super vibrant red—I call it "little old lady red," which was really popular in the 1950s. Get the cheapest version of that, and you'll have a lipstick that will stay on forever. Even after you take it off, you'll see the stain marks on your skin. You can dull it down with your brown foundation if you want to make it look like a scab or do some sort of blood effect with it. You don't have to worry about it sweating off, and it's cheap, which is the whole point.

I mentioned sponges, and another thing that's fun is to get natural sponges or stipple sponges. You can lightly dab those in makeup and then plop those on your face to create all kinds of texture. All this stuff is cheap, cheap, cheap. You have to take a little bit of time to learn how to use the makeup and tools, and, as I said, creativity will provide—including for those who only have a tiny amount of money to invest.

New Uses for Common Foods

Another great tool is either spirit gum (a skin adhesive) or liquid latex. In a pinch, you can even use eyelash glue. You can just glue stuff to your face and cover it with your makeup. This creates texture, and you don't have to invest in high-end prosthetics that you have to learn how to mold. If you're using liquid latex, and you want to make it appear as though your brains are popping out of your forehead, you can put a layer of latex down and glue some elbow macaroni to your forehead. Then take a torn paper towel, tissue paper, or Kleenex soaked in liquid latex and put that around the macaroni so it looks like the skin is peeling away and the brains are emerging. Paint over the macaroni with latex so it all stays in place, dab it with some pink and red, and you've got brains coming out of your forehead.

I had a friend in college who was a theater student. He'd paint spirit gum on his lower face and dab coffee grounds onto the spirit gum to give him a five o'clock shadow. He'd do this when he was trying to get into bars and wasn't old enough. Apparently, it worked, or they just thought, "Here's somebody crazy enough to glue coffee to his face, so let's let him in. He could probably use a drink."

Another thing that's fun to use is cornflakes or other dry cereal. Crunch it up and use that liquid latex to apply the cereal to your face. You can make it look like road rash where the skin has peeled off and you've got asphalt embedded in your skin. Just play with it. Take a night that you're not doing anything, call your friends, and say, "Hey, bring something stupid I can glue to your face, and we'll see how it works."

When I was in college, I actually did an entire clown makeup using nothing but liquid latex and yarn. I took different-colored yarn and glued it in a spiral out from the center, so each strand of yarn was right next to the other. I created round cheeks, I put it around my mouth in three different colors, and I put it around my eyes. When you're working with latex, it's always good to use a blow dryer to dry the latex. Have it set on cool—otherwise, it hurts. You can get a blow dryer at pretty much any thrift store. The heating mechanism doesn't even need to work, because you'll never use that.

Here's an idea I stole from drag queens for making it look like your eyebrows have either been shaved or you never had them, which comes in really handy if you're doing aliens or people in asylums. You can do this with eyebrow wax, but there's no point in investing in that because you want something cheap that works really well. You can get a washable glue stick that goes on purple but dries clear. Work that into your eyebrows, and then take a tiny eyebrow brush or comb and use that to smooth your eyebrows down against your brow. Once the glue dries, your eyebrows are flat and smooth. You put foundation makeup over the top of them, and then draw eyebrows above where your actual eyebrows are/were. This also works for clown makeup.

Terrific Blood Recipes

Of course, everyone wants blood. I'm sure everyone has their own favorite blood recipe, and most blood you can create from ingredients available at a grocery store. My favorite blood recipe is dark corn syrup to which a couple of drops of red and a quarter to a half as many drops of blue food coloring—say four or five drops of red and a drop of blue—are added. I like to use dark corn syrup because I like blood that's darker in color—richer and browner. If you like bright red blood, you can use light corn syrup. My favorite thing to add at the end is just a little sprinkling of cocoa powder. It makes the blood taste better if you're using it in your mouth, and it also makes it a little more opaque.

You can make up enough of this blood to do an entire cast for maybe four or five bucks, max. Of course, you can't buy food coloring by the drop. You have to buy it by the bottle. You may have everything you need in your kitchen, right now, to make blood. You can make a little blood capsule, pop that into your mouth, and bite down on it. That can be fun.

Finding Free Props

Now we're going to talk about props. One of the things I've had great luck with is using my computer to find public-domain images—things like train tickets, old posters, and other things that have fallen into the public domain, which means nobody owns the rights to these, and you don't have to pay to use them. There are entire websites dedicated to public-domain images, video, literature, or music, so you can search for any of these public-domain properties. Even certain classic movies have fallen into public domain. You can put that imagery, video, or whatever on your computer, print it, and make your own props.

Which brings up another tip—invest in a printer. A lot of people don't have printers anymore, but you need one. It doesn't have to be a high-end printer, but it does have to be a color printer. You can print up so many wonderful props. For example, in The Vault of Souls, we had one hallway with death certificates plastered to the wall. Those were all printed on my computer. I wrote them all, and I put the names of people I knew would be visiting on them. Instead of investing a ton of money in paint, we invested a ton of money in wallpaper paste, which we used to paste up all these printed-up death certificates. They were very cool, and personalized.

You can also do handwritten notes. If guests take them or they get destroyed, you can print 20 of them and only use one at a time. This is a great, cheap way to add unique props that tell your story.

The Importance of Investing in Hero Props

Although there are tons of ways to do things on the cheap, there are some things you shouldn't skimp on. I'm a firm believer that you should invest in a few what I'll call hero props, hero masks, or hero costumes. These are the things that are visible to guests for long periods of time. Most haunt actors are only seen for a few seconds before they disappear back into the darkness. However, for queue-line characters or characters that are seen for longer periods of time by guests, this is where you want to spend your money. Invest in a great silicon mask for a clown that people will see for a long period of time. The next clown, which will only be seen for a few seconds, can have a mud mask, white powder, and cheap lipstick, and guests will perceive the same level of quality they just saw in the silicone mask.

So, do spend money on key pieces of scenic, costumes, and props. Find those hero items, and make sure they're properly lit if people see them for a long period of time, because they'll perceive everything they see to be of that same quality. The mind automatically does that.

In summary, there's always a way to make something happen on a budget. Make it cheap, make it fast, make it good—pick two. Make sure you've got enough time to make it cheap and good because you're going to be doing a lot of work. Make sure you create a plan based on what you know you can execute—in other words, write your story based on the location you're in, what you have, and what you can get a hold of, and find ways to make those things work cohesively. If you do that, these tips will help you be a more cost-effective haunter so you can either put more money into your home haunt or put more money into your pocket if you have a professional haunt.

PART THREE

THE HAUNT COMMUNITY

Chapter 12

The Pros and Cons of Shows and Cons

The last two chapters of this book focus on your haunt in the context of the larger haunt community. In this chapter, we'll discuss how to decide which events and shows to attend and why they're important to you and your haunt. I'll be talking about trade shows, seminars, symposiums, and other cons.

Three Excellent Events for Haunters to Attend

I'm going to begin with three excellent and varied events for haunters to attend.

Seasonal Entertainment Source *Leadership Symposium*

As I mentioned earlier, I was lucky enough to be one of the keynote speakers at the *Seasonal Entertainment Source* [formerly *The Haunt Journal*] Leadership Symposium held at Knott's Berry Farm in 2018. This symposium was a great meeting of the minds. I got to sit on a panel with several of my heroes—among them, Ricky Briganti and Margee Kerr. It was very well attended, and there were a whole bunch of people that I got to chat with as well.

The people on this panel had a ton of experience, and the theme of this symposium was innovation in immersive theater and immersive techniques. There were people there representing The Queen Mary, people who worked at Netherworld, people who'd worked at Eastern State Penitentiary, and then Ricky, who's been to pretty much every single haunt in the world and was there to talk about Shadow's Fall and The Republic. I was there representing The Vault of Souls and my work with Howl-O-Scream many years ago at Busch Gardens. We each spoke for about 20 minutes—it was sort of like Ted Talks for haunters. Then there was a question-and-answer session, which was moderated by my friend, Leonard Pickel, the Hauntrepreneur himself.

For anyone in the haunt industry or who's thinking about it, the Leadership Symposium is a great place to get a bunch of information. These happen each year. Go to the Haunted Attraction Network website, www.hauntedattractionnetwork.com, to find out when the next Symposium takes place.

Midsummer Scream

Another show I went to while I was on the West Coast was Midsummer Scream. That was a completely different kind of event but so very much fun. It was just a blast—a great amalgam of haunt and horror fans and haunt industry folks. There was something for everybody.

I guess you could call Midsummer Scream a con, but I think they call it a Halloween festival or a celebration of Halloween in July. Who's not going to go to that? I'm certainly going to be there. The cool thing about bringing together haunt fans, the haunt industry, and creating a show that appeals to both is that haunters are or were haunt fans, too. We're all fanboys or fangirls at one time or another, and I think it's really important to bring those two sides together.

Midsummer Scream is an interesting show because not only did it have haunt vendors but there were classes, symposiums, and presentations by everything from the Knott's Scary Farm team to the Halloween Haunt team to a group doing radio drama based on the old *Tales From The Crypt* comic books, which was super cool. I got to see a bunch of things I'd never seen before and, being on the opposite side of the country, in Florida, it was nice to see what was happening in the Pacific time zone.

Midsummer Scream also featured two- to three-room samples of various attractions' haunt or haunted experience in what's known as The Hall of Shadows. Guests had the opportunity to go through and experience a taster of what these haunts had to offer. Boy, was that inspiring!

Urban Death

Another show I'd strongly recommend if you're really twisted, over the age of 18, and not easily offended, is Urban Death, which I'd never experienced before. This is a production of Zombie Joes' Underground Theater Group, and it was one of the weirdest things I've ever seen. Some people didn't care for it at all because it was just so odd, but I loved every minute of it. It involved short vignettes that had everything from monsterish puppet creations to full-frontal nudity. It just pushed all the buttons and bars. There was everything from cute carved pumpkins to a guy doing something inappropriate to a cute carved pumpkin. We'll just leave it at that. In addition, there was a cat-adoption area in which kitties needing homes were roaming through a cemetery, which I thought was adorable.

"Why Should I Go?"

I'm guessing everybody who's reading this has been to—or at least thought about going to—one or another of the various and sundry tradeshows that happen around the country each year, everything from the Transworld Show in Saint Louis to HAuNTCon to Midwest Haunters to Chicago Frights to ScareLA and a number of other haunt-based shows.

If you haven't gone to one, you're probably asking, "Why should I go?" It's an investment of both time and money, so I'm going to tell you why I go.

For me, the most important reason is, I like to meet people. Now, having been in the haunt industry for [mumble] years, I'm lucky enough to know quite a few people, and I get to see them, hang out with them, and go to dinner with them—which I did with Leonard and his wife, Jeanne, as well as my friends Kyle and Tater. We went to an escape room one night and had dinner the following night. These shows are a wonderful networking opportunity. It's a great chance to meet folks you might only be friends with on Facebook. It's also a chance to meet folks who do podcasts, because they're usually there making some sort of appearance.

It's also a great way to share ideas. I've been going to the Transworld show for probably 20 years now. I used to go when it was in Chicago, and then I went when it was in Vegas. The thing about that particular show is, not only do you get to go out on this massive tradeshow floor, which is like a candy store for every haunter, but more important than that to me is the camaraderie of sitting around before or after the show or at one of the sponsored events and talking with people and sharing ideas. Back in the day in Chicago, everyone would gather in the lobby of the Holiday Inn, because that's where most of the haunters were staying, and talk about things. You'd see all kinds of monsters and creatures walk through this lobby, because it was right next to the convention center, and it was affordable, so almost everybody stayed there.

One night, the team from Universal Studios in Florida, Halloween Horror Nights, and Lowry Park Zoo in Tampa were there along with a couple of other vendors, and we were just sitting around and coming up with the coolest ideas. It's the best brainstorming place in the world to talk about what might happen next in the haunt industry—or, more specifically, what's going to happen next in your haunt. Folks in the haunt industry are very willing to chat and share ideas. If they're not, they should be.

I mentioned the haunt samples in The Hall of Shadows. Seeing and hearing about other people's work can either reinforce what you're doing or give you ideas about how you can expand. In my opinion, if you're inspired by someone else, and you can do something as well or better or in a different way, do it. There are no new ideas, just different ways to put the existing ones together. So, go out and get as much inspiration as you can by seeing other people's haunted attractions.

You'll Be the First to Know about New Haunt Products

The other thing about these events is you'll be the first to see—and touch—new products in the haunt industry. You're not just seeing them on a website—you get to hold them and ask the vendor questions about them. In many cases, the vendor will be able to adapt them for your specific needs. You might ask things like, "Can you paint this mask with UV? Can you take the blood off this particular prop, because we're doing a kid-friendly event—or, can you add more blood to it, because we're nowhere near kid-friendly?" When you can to talk to the vendors, if they make their own stuff, they'll often be more than happy to customize it for you. There may be an additional fee, obviously, but sometimes there isn't. If you want something they don't offer but they have something similar, you can say to them, "I want a rhinoceros ghost. Can you build a rhinoceros ghost for me?" If anybody does build a rhinoceros ghost, I'd like to see it, so please send me a picture of that.

Network, Network, Network

So, when you go to these shows, what should you plan to do? Each show has its own personality. Some shows are more party-heavy than others, and some are more focused on education, practicum, make-and-takes, and that sort of thing. Do some research on the shows that interest you, so you know what they're about.

However, first and foremost, as I said before, you want to network. Since you're going to want to chat with anyone and everyone, make sure you have some form of business card. I realize business cards are probably going by the wayside. Pretty soon, we'll just be able to shake hands and instantly people's contact information will electronically go into our devices—if the technology isn't there already. But, until that time comes, bring business cards with you. You can get some inexpensively and quickly online at VistaPrint.com, or Zazzle.com does business cards as well.

As a vendor, of course, there are people you want to get in front of. I realize it costs some additional money for vendors to rent the space and transport their merchandise, etc. Some shows don't allow you to sell on the tradeshow floor, but what better way to take orders? It opens you up to people you've not had business contacts with before. So, with vendors, too, it's an opportunity to network, network, network.

Be prepared to share your ideas and listen to other people's input. If you've got something halfway planned, you can be vague enough that nobody will steal your idea before you get it out there. Besides, chances are you're going to be talking to people who aren't necessarily in your market. It's like having a very knowledgeable brainstorming team. You can ask them, "Have you guys ever tried anything with exploding tarot cards?" Once again, if you've tried anything with exploding tarot cards, please send me a photo. Share those ideas with people. You'll get responses ranging from, "That's a great idea," to, "Yeah, we tried that, but we put too much gasoline in them, and the guests caught on fire." They'll tell you what's worked for them and what hasn't. People like to listen to other people's ideas and to plan haunts, even if they're not their own.

When you get there, be prepared to reach out to folks you don't know. Go say hi to somebody you've never met. Find out who they are and what they do. Don't do it with the thought of, "I hope I can get work from this person." Do it from the mindset of, "Here's somebody who's like-minded and cares about the haunt industry the way I do, or they wouldn't be here." So, they may become a business associate, they become a client, they may become a vendor for you, or they may just become a friend. It doesn't matter. All of these things are positive. Sit at a table with people you don't know. If you're hesitant, grab one of your friends and say, "Hey, let's go sit at that table, introduce ourselves, and start talking with them." This is super easy to do it at most of the shows, festivals, and events out there.

Take Plenty of Photos

Don't forget to take tons of photos—but only of what you're allowed to photograph, of course. Each show, festival, and con has different rules about what you can take photos of. If you're on a tradeshow floor, always ask the vendor before you take a photograph. If you're visiting a haunt, chances are good they won't want you to take pictures inside, so take plenty of pictures outside. At all the parties or in the lobby, take as many pictures as you possibly can, and share them on social media. Recently, I was able to post things from different shows—or different parts of different shows—on social media to let people know what was going on and hopefully inspire them to attend next year. Oh, and don't forget to take an extra battery pack and remember to charge your phone every night.

Attend Parties

Almost every convention or event has some sort of sponsored party. If you don't know anyone at the event, a great way to get immediately into the scene is to go to one of the sponsored parties. These are usually masquerade parties, which makes them even more fun. Hang out, get to know people, network, and have a good time.

Don't Forget Your Credit Card

Bring some extra cash or a credit card that still has room on it, because, I promise you, you'll want to buy something while you're on that tradeshow floor. Some companies go to the bigger shows like Transworld and buy everything for their event at that tradeshow—every single thing. You have to plan this out before you get there. Have some idea of what your theme is going to be, what you're going to add, or what you want to replace before you go to the show. Usually, you can get great deals at tradeshows. Many vendors will offer a show deal or a show discount of some sort. You can also negotiate with them for things like a reduction in shipping costs or a volume discount. So, if you have the requirements for your haunt in mind, the tradeshow floor can be the best place to make those purchases.

Conversely, you can go with an open mind and use what's available on the tradeshow floor as inspiration. It can work both ways. In my experience, you get the best pricing deal if you're able to purchase or place your order while you're on the floor itself.

Review the Contacts You Made

After you get home from a trade show, sort through the business cards you collected, because you'll have a stack of them. Sort through those cards and put them into your contacts. If you have one of those fancy apps on your phone where you can take a picture of the business card and it automatically puts it into your contacts, use it. These are people you want to be able to contact right away if you need them, and you never know when that will be. If there was somebody you really liked or had a good chat with, send them an email or add them on Facebook. I have tons of Facebook friends I met at shows. They're the people who are going to look at the photos you post from the next show you attend and say, "Oh my gosh, that looks like so much fun. I wish I could be there with you." And, the following year, they will be.

The Advantages of Attending a Parallel Industry Tradeshow

Attending a parallel industry tradeshow that isn't specifically about horror and haunting but offers related information and experiences is a great way to get inspired. To this end, I attended The Special Event show that took place on January 8-10, 2019 at the San Diego Convention Center in California. Although this wasn't a haunt tradeshow, I was lucky enough to present a seminar on incorporating atmospheric entertainment into large-scale events and festivals. This was the first time I'd ever been to this show, and the only reason I was there was because one of my clients, Zoo Tampa, thought this would be a good show for me. So, I applied to present and ended up teaching a seminar. There were over 100 people in attendance at my seminar. I asked myself, "Who would want to come to a talk by a haunter geek at a special event?" But there was a great response. It was an absolutely phenomenal tradeshow, and I was glad my seminar went well.

Be Present When You're There

I attended a number of seminars while I was there. One of them was on how to get the most out of this The Special Event show, and it was good information for pretty much any convention you go to, whether it's a haunt show or any con or tradeshow. The most important thing was, make sure you're present. Don't spend your entire time at the tradeshow on your phone. It's an investment to come to tradeshows, so be there when you're there. Set up time outside the tradeshow to do your work if you need to do work, but be present at the show. You've paid to be there, so don't waste your money.

The other thing that was brought up was using this event as a networking opportunity—meet people, talk to them, attend various and sundry social gatherings, and, if you're waiting in line for something and you see somebody in front of you who has a nametag or lanyard for the event, make sure you talk to them and introduce yourself. This was especially important for me, because this was my first time at this show, and special events isn't necessarily the kind of industry I'm familiar with. I've done special events but for theme parks, zoos, aquariums, and that sort of thing, so they were more like festivals. The folks at this show were everything from wedding planners to big corporate planners, so I didn't know anybody there.

A speaker at another seminar pointed out that it's important to be aware of everything any tradeshow has to offer you. The reason I'm sharing this information is because this is a golden opportunity for anybody. If you're planning to go to any of the haunt shows—HAuNTcon, Transworld, Midwest, Midsummer Scream, or any of the haunt conventions—all of these have great information. Participate, walk up to people that you may have seen online, and say, "Hi, I'm so-and-so." It's important to say hello, because, just like at this event, the haunt tradeshows are just as open to people chatting with you. I know I certainly am!

So, take advantage of the show itself, be present, and be a participant. I was happy to hear this is true in pretty much every industry, not just haunting. Everybody knows that haunters are a great big family, but the folks in the special-event world also refer to themselves as a great big family.

I've always said that the majority of business at a haunt convention is done in the bar, but I think it's important to attend the seminars and educate yourself, even if it's a topic you don't think is going to be of interest. Expanding your knowledge really helps you.

A Seminar on First Impressions Confirms My Views

Another seminar I attended at The Special Event show was all about first impressions. This was covered in a 2019 issue of *Seasonal Entertainment Source*, to which I contributed an article on this topic. So, I decided to attend a seminar presented by someone on the exact same topic to see if I could polish my views. What was really fascinating to me was, the speaker said pretty much all the same stuff I said. She expanded it a little bit more and focused more on brand—not just personal interaction but also email interaction and website interaction. It was really nice to not only have my views reinforced but to learn a more about something that's near and dear to my heart.

Presenting and Serving Food that Integrates with the Event Theme

Then I went to the opening-night party. When a special-event show does an opening-night party, they pull out all the stops. I was thrilled that much of what I'd been talking about in my seminar regarding atmospheric entertainment and the different purposes it serves in a special event were all demonstrated at this party. It took place on an aircraft carrier and was themed to the 1940s. And, there was this amazing food. There were caterers there providing not only different samplings of food but also different ways of serving it.

So, I got to thinking that this is something haunters need to know. When you decide to put culinary into your mix as a way to earn revenue, make sure it's displayed in an interesting way. For example, haunters could display cotton candy in bags clipped to a giant spider web. Obviously, you could serve stuff in coffins and cauldrons. There's a whole bunch of opportunities there.

A Different Photo Op and Other Unique Ideas for Haunts

On the second day at The Special Event show, I had an opportunity to see the tradeshow floor. I have to say, it was so much fun to go to a tradeshow where I've never seen the vendors before. Having gone to the haunt shows for so many years, it's always kind of, "Let's see what the returning folks have that's new, and let's see what new folks are here." For the most part, it's going back and seeing the same stuff over and over again, so I can go through the tradeshow floors pretty quickly. This one was roughly the size of a HAuNTtcon tradeshow floor, and it had such interesting vendors that were all new to me. There were laser vendors doing some fun laser stuff and a lot of photography vendors who were taking photos.

That got me thinking. Why aren't there more photograph options at haunted attractions? I think everybody has selfie stations and uses them for promotional purposes, but these guys were actually taking photos, and some of them were high-end and professional. They posted them via the Internet or emailed them. So, they weren't only taking photos and providing opportunities to guests, they were gathering data—email addresses—to build a communication database, which I thought was a really cool idea. You could sell those photos as well. Add a monster in there, have your photographer take a quality monster portrait, and email it to the guest. You don't have to worry about printing costs, and you don't have to worry about much overhead. You could have everybody repost it on their social media to promote your haunt on a media night, preview night, or special VIP night of some sort.

Another thing I saw on the tradeshow floor that was unique and could be applied to the haunt industry were these cool, inflatable, character costumes. One was a giant white dragon in which a performer provided the two back legs and another performer puppeteered the head on a long neck. This could work really well in a haunt, especially in a blackout house or 3D house—an inflatable character that comes to life and doesn't have to hide behind anything. If you put the puppeteer handling the head into a black morph suit, make everything else blacklight-reactive, and paint it with 3D paint, that would be a new twist for a 3D or Chromadepth house.

A Seminar on Storytelling

I also went to a seminar that was all about storytelling. Most of you know this is the number-one thing I love to talk about—the importance of telling a good story. This was presented by the guy who does events for the MGM hotels in Las Vegas, and he was talking about everything you've heard me talk about. First, have a good story with a beginning, middle, and end. This helps give you focus and helps make the emotional impact much stronger, whatever you're doing. He was taking everything I've always talked about related to storytelling and making it applicable to the special-event industry.

What's Old Is New—in a Different Venue

Sort of switching topics here for a moment, there's a lot of really cool technology out there that isn't horribly expensive—or, at least, it won't be horribly expensive in another year or two—and which haunters should grab on to as soon as they can. At The Special Event show, there were a couple pieces of programmable LED lighting equipment that were really neat. There were a few robot things, including one that looked like a cross between Wall-E and Johnny 5. (If you know who Johnny 5 is, you're my age.) It had a camera in its face, a screen in its chest, and it was controlled by a remote operator who was standing out of the guest's sightline as the robot approached them. He wasn't only creating the movement of this robot but also the voice. The robot was able to take pictures and generate video—again, another way to connect to people's social-media accounts.

On the third day of this event, I was back on the tradeshow floor. I saw things that were considered new to the event industry that haunters and theme parks have been using for years and years. That was a real eye-opener. One thing we've been using in haunted attractions is Chromadepth glasses or Chromadepth technology for 3D—more specifically, those little light-point or point-source hologram glasses, the ones where when you look at any light point and it throws an image around it like a heart or a logo or a phrase or a skull or whatever. We've been using these in theme parks for at least 15 or 20 years, but they were one of the new things for special events.

Another thing I thought was an interesting adaptation was the vortex tunnel. They're now doing this with curved, LED video monitors, which gives you significantly more options but is also significantly higher priced.

Although this probably wouldn't apply too much to the haunt industry, SkyFire Arts does a fire and lightning show in which three performers wear basically chainmail, are grounded, and shoot lightning at one another. They also shoot pyro. If you have an outdoor haunt or an outdoor queue or an outdoor performance area where a lot of people gather before or after your haunt, this would be a really cool show to have. It would light up in a nighttime venue.

A Virtual-Reality Dining Experience and Other Discoveries

What else was there that I thought was fascinating? There was a really interesting experience called Sublimotion, which is a virtual-reality dining experience. It's probably the most expensive dinner you'll ever have. You go into a white room and, with each course, the projections on the walls change the environment. You wear VR glasses for part of the meal, and there's projection mapping on your plate. It was the most high-tech fantasy dinner I've ever seen. The idea is clearly way beyond the budget of most haunters, but using special-effects technology to create a dinner was pretty cool. So, haunters, if you want to use the various technological things we use in our haunts—projections, monitors, light programs, air cannons, and that sort of thing—to create a seance dinner, ghost dinner, or other kind of dining experience that tells a story, this would be very cool as an upcharge—probably for theme-park haunts or larger scream parks.

However, just about anybody could do this by adding food to their haunt—not just hot dogs and hamburgers but an actual, sit-down meal—that thematically ties in. You can use your special effects to have a projected ghost flying around the table or the room as guests eat or have a video monitor in a frame that comes to life to announce the next course. This is technology we already use. This is a new way of looking at it and approaching it.

There was a company there called Atomic Design that had a lot of really cool fabric backdrops. They started in the concert industry, but now their real bread and butter is high-end special events. Their products are both rentable and purchasable. Check them out. Again, they're not inexpensive, but just looking at what they have might give you ideas for unique textures for your walls and your backdrops, so guests aren't looking past a scene at the brick wall of your building. They use stretch spandex to create scenic shapes, projection surfaces, and backdrops in general. I'm not sure what the application might be for haunters, but I think there's something there that's worth looking into.

There was a company called TLC Creative that had what they call water tubes, which are essentially internal fountains. Think of a giant test tube inverted over the top of a single-shoot fountain with LED lights at the bottom. If you're doing any sort of sci-fi or just want to do some sort of cool, mad-scientist's lab, these things are really neat. I'm sure the MacGyvers out there could figure out a way to construct these themselves and make them significantly more cost-effective. These were nine-feet tall and amazing.

Then I saw a device that was kinda weird and kinda sad at the same time. It might be cool if you're a real technogeek. A company is using facial-recognition software to chart the emotional response of an audience by focusing on 75 people and mapping certain indices on the face—like when the eyebrows go up or the brow furrows or whatever—and matching that to an emotion to produce a graph that shows, for example, when the audience was engaged but there was no emotional content, when they were marginally engaged but very emotional, or both.

I say, just watch and listen to your audience. This is a high-tech company that spent a lot of money developing this, and I'm sure large corporations will eat it up. My thought is, we can do this by watching the crowd and certainly by standing at the exit of our haunt and listening to what people say as they come out. We won't have a cool chart and a fun piece of software to play with, but we can do just as much by watching and paying attention to our audiences.

Another cool item was Chat Bands. These are LED wrist bands to which you can send programmable messages in real time. This might have an interesting application in the escape-room industry. Just like Gantom Torch has created individually programmed flashlights that do different things for different people, with these Chat Bands, you could send different messages to different people. You could send a clue to one person in the group, and they could relay it to the other people in the group.

A company called Fun4Events offers a temporary-tattoo printer that takes an image—like a logo or anything you can think of—and prints it as a temporary tattoo directly on the skin. I don't know if this is an upcharge opportunity or a marketing opportunity, but, knowing haunters and their affinity for tattoos, it could be a popular item. There are tons of haunters who have phenomenal skin art, and this would be like the training-wheels version of that. It also gives you the opportunity to put your brand or your logo on someone's skin, and they walk around with that. The tattoo is removed with rubbing alcohol, just like any other temporary tattoo.

Keep Your Eyes, Ears, and Mind Open

The take-home for me from this event was, even if you don't think a particular tradeshow has something to offer you, be open to it, be open to learning, and be open to being a student. It was great to come to this show and not know all the key players, not know the successes and failures of the special-event industry, and find ways to make new friends, new business associates, etc. For those of you who are haunters, don't limit yourself.

People say all the time, "I wish I could do a seasonal haunt that goes on for 12 months." There are some people who can do that, and that's great if you're in a market that will bear that, but it's a challenge for the majority of folks. What became apparent to me in attending this conference is we need to keep our eyes open and keep our options open to find ways to utilize our expertise in a new market. Don't just think haunts have to happen around Halloween. The way we control guests, the way we control emotions, the way we control the flow of people through an atmospheric experience like a haunted house or an escape room can be applied to many different scenarios in many industries. Anything you learn can be applied to a haunt, or anything in a haunt can be applied to other things. That was the eye-opening takeaway from this.

A Great Opportunity to Share Information with Professionals in Another Area

I was supposed to go to the awards ceremony on the final night, but I had the opportunity to go out to dinner with two new friends I met at the show. As important as the tradeshow floor is, as important as the seminars are, the most important thing is making new friends and sharing information with real professionals who are already doing this. I think that's true of any tradeshow you go to. I believe most of my time should be spent hanging out with people, learning from my peers, and reaching out to share stories: "We did this when we had such-and-such a problem. How would you handle this situation?" That's the biggest benefit from tradeshows. Whether it's in your industry or in a parallel industry, that's really the lesson to keep in mind.

"Is It Worth It?"

Another question that people often ask me is, "Is it worth it to go to these shows? Is it worth it to spend all that time?" There's only one answer to that, which is "Yes." Yes, it's completely worth it. You're surrounded by a bunch of like-minded people and, at certain conventions, it's just one big party—often with lots of alcohol. There are parties that happen in the hotel rooms and various and sundry suites. If you don't know which conventions those are, ask the folks that go to lots of conventions which ones are the party conventions.

These events aren't only fun, they're important to the development and ongoing growth of your haunt or your understanding of the haunt industry. Make attending these events part of your haunt budget—the marketing budget, the research-and-development budget, or whatever line item will allow you to squeak out some extra money. That way, when the event rolls around, you don't have to worry about whether you have the funds or not. Budget it and book early, if you can. Most conventions, festivals, and events have partner hotels that will give better deals on rooms. When festivals and events offer those kinds of hotel deals, they're not necessarily packages. Another thing you can do is schedule your vacation around the event. If you're planning on taking an annual vacation, spend two days of it at Transworld, two days at HAuNTcon, a few days at Midsummer Scream, ScareLA, Spooky Empire, or any of the other haunt conventions. If you're going someplace cool for a convention, there's always something else cool to do there.

I make these events part of my budgeted expenses for my business, because I think it's essential for me to be at these places to continue to be on the cutting edge, to meet potential clients, and to share my ideas. One thing that's important to me is to continue to keep the haunt industry growing, coming up with new ideas, and not stagnating. Whenever I attend these events, it's always the case that I see something I've never seen before, or I come up with a great idea while having coffee with so-and-so. I've met people from all over the world at these conventions, and it's completely worth it. Find the money. Just find the money.

Maybe you can't fly across the country to an event, but there are local gatherings of haunters in many places. Often, they're gathering to do make-and-takes. They'll come together, make a prop, talk about ideas, and then go home. See what's around you locally, and start with those. Later on, you can go to one of the larger cons. Many change their venue each year. HAuNTcon, for example, has been everywhere from Orlando to Nashville to Birmingham to New Orleans. So, you can keep an eye out for when it's coming to a city near you.

If you don't have a con coming to a city near you, start one. Only do this if you have a ton of extra time, because they're a huge amount of work, and there's a lot that goes into them. I've never hosted one myself, but I have friends who have. It's a bit of a financial risk, because you do have to invest a lot of money up front. If you're passionate about it, do it. Contact me, and I'll do my best to attend and have a great time at whatever your convention is.

The Big Question— Which Show to Attend

With all the events, all the cons, and all the other shows out there, which are the best shows to go to? I have no idea how to answer that question, because each one of us is going to want to get something different from a show. If you're on the fan side of things, there are shows that are focused on the different horror brands out there. There are celebrities signing autographs and great artists creating beautiful work. I was at one show—maybe an escape-room show—not long ago, and that's where I got the three, beautiful, hand-drawn charcoal pieces of artwork of Edgar Allan Poe, the Raven, and the Black Cat that now hang in my office. You'll find that sort of thing at shows that target haunt and horror fans.

There are shows that aren't necessarily haunt-related that might benefit you. MegaCon, DragonCon, or some of the sci-fi conventions or gory horror-film conventions could be worthwhile for certain people.

Then, of course, there are the shows that focus more on the professional haunter or the home haunter. I have to say that the Transworld show is by far the quintessential MacDaddy of these shows. That's the one where you'll find pretty much anything you can imagine. It's focused primarily on the haunter, not the haunt fan, but there's plenty there for the haunt fan as well.

Do some research and decide what it is you're looking for and where you're going to get the most bang for your buck. There are a ton of shows I haven't mentioned, just because I can't remember them right now. Go online, do some research, talk to friends who've been to different shows, and listen to what they have to say. Maybe plan a road trip together. I know people who go to almost every single one of these shows. They all pile into a van—10 haunters in a van. The journey can be even more fun than the event itself, but make sure it's not so much fun that you don't remember why you went there or what you experienced while you were there. This is another reason to take lots of pictures—it helps you remember.

Chapter 13

When the Blood Flows, All Haunts Rise

Now, for our last chapter, lucky number 13, I'm going to talk about how each of us can help our own haunt by helping build up the haunt industry. I've seen a lot of trash talk online about different haunted attractions and people associated with those haunted attractions, and I'm going to talk about why it's important not to do that.

Let's face it, there's enough ugliness in the world right now, and we don't need to be throwing shade at other haunters or people we've worked with before. This might be something of a preachy chapter, so I'm just going to warn you a little beforehand that I'm going to be getting up on my soapbox. So, sit down, relax, and let me get this out of my system, because it's important.

Stop the Trash Talk

There's a reason why there's so much trash talk in the haunt industry and why there are so many people out there saying, "My haunt is better than your haunt," or, "You don't do crap." Whether it's creative differences, business differences, or competitive differences doesn't matter. We shouldn't be saying negative things publicly about one another.

But we do, and here's why I think that happens. We're all so passionate about what we do in the haunt industry that we want to share that passion…and our opinions. That's why I do a podcast and publish a blog—because I want to share my passion about the haunt industry. With that passion comes a certain amount of territorialism, which expresses itself as "my haunt is better than your haunt." Due to our nature, we form a competition so one of us can win, and we feel the only way for one of us to win is for somebody to lose. However, there's not a finite amount of winning available in this world.

In that light, think about it before you get online and post, "XYZ haunt sucks because of this, this, and this," or, "XYZ haunter did this or did that." This hurts all of us, as an industry, and I know I sound like a hippie singing "Kumbaya," but it's true—it hurts us all as an industry. When our industry doesn't show a united front and demonstrate that we support one another, we're making ourselves look bad and stupid. We're making us all look like amateurs, and we're not. We're professional haunters, and haunting is a profession, so treat it as such.

Whenever you say something about somebody else's haunt, make sure it's true—which a lot of the stuff I've been seeing recently online is not. It's either completely false or an extremely biased perspective, let's put it that way. Some of it is true, but let's not air it publicly, you know? If you have a problem with someone, contact them directly so you can work it out. When you put it out there in a public forum, it's not just hurting the industry as a whole, it's hurting you as an individual.

Not Only Does Your Reputation Suffer, So Does the Industry

I was told a long time ago to never date someone who's cheating on their current lover to be with you, because they'll cheat on you to be with somebody else. I apply that theory to the business world as well. If a potential employer sees somebody online who's pissing and moaning about their previous employer, previous haunt, or previous circumstance, that employer is going to look at them very carefully and say, "If they did this in the past, they might do it to me if I hire them." It hurts your reputation when you're negative in a public forum. People don't want to work with you.

So, You Want to Be a Full-Time Haunter...

I get a lot of emails from people who say, "I want to be a full-time haunter." Let's face it, there are zero people I know who are full-time haunters, who do haunt as their only job. Well, that's not completely true. There are full-time haunters, but they're few and far between. We all recognize that. I'm not a full-time haunter. My heart is in haunt, but I do a lot of different things as an entertainment consultant. Around Halloween, the majority of those things have to do with haunted attractions, but the rest of the year I'm working on everything from Christmas to summer events to theater productions to whatever interesting project comes my way that I can say yes to. I'm all about that.

When people contact me and say they want to be a full-time haunter, after I stop laughing, my answer is usually very simple—"Well, then haunt." But I should probably change that to, "Well, then haunt—because the only way you're going to get to do it is to say you're going to get to do it, and, hopefully, eventually, someone will pay you for it or you'll make money with it. If not, you're still doing it." And I should probably add to the end of that, "Haunt, and don't piss people off."

No matter how good a haunter you are or how brilliant your product is, ultimately, it comes down to whether somebody wants to work with you or not. I hate to admit it, but there are a lot of people out there who have the same skill level and experience as the rest of us. None of us are extraordinarily unique in our experience or in our talent. We may be very good at what we do, we may have strengths other people don't have, but, there's a level where it's not about—or not as much about—what you know and what your experience is as it is about how much people want to work with you.

Let me be transparent. I'm longer at Busch Gardens because I wasn't brave enough to leave on my own, so I have to thank the company over and over for doing their restructuring. Ever since I left, the only thing that continues to get me work is my integrity. That's really the only thing you take with you throughout your entire career. It's not about your resumé, it's not about your skill set, it's about your integrity.

If You're Looking for Work, Be Someone Who Fits with the Culture

I was recently at an event in Tampa, and I was sitting next to a woman who's a human-resources representative. She knows nothing about the haunted attraction industry, and we were talking about hiring practices and hiring people. She commented, "You want to hire the right person for the culture, someone who's going to fit in, someone who's not going to tick people off, and someone who'll work well with the rest of the team." I can promise you, if you're that guy or gal out there griping about, "I was cheated by so-and-so," or "such-and-such haunt sucks," or "I worked with so-and-so, and they were a complete jerk," you're not going to be viewed as a person who'll work within the culture. I'd assume this is true if you're applying for a job outside the haunt industry as well.

Whether we like to admit it or not, social media is being used by human-resources departments to do research on people. It's a heck of a lot cheaper than doing a background check, and you can find an awful lot about people online. I know my life is pretty much out there—and not just the good stuff. There are stupid things I've done that still pop up online. That's why it's so very important for us, as a community, to say, "We're not going to diss each other. We're not going to do it."

I want to start some sort of clever and creative hashtag like #playnice or #haunterssupporthaunters, but I'm not sure that's going to make a difference. If you want to use one of these, great.

Speak Up Against Negativity

I've been involved with a lot of different presentations and events—Robbiween and stuff like that—where haunters come together to help other haunters. It's important to not just do that at the big festivals but in our everyday lives. Even if you're not the person starting some sort of comment chain about who did what to whom, don't chime in. Just like with other forms of inappropriate behavior, sometimes you have to step up and say, "That's not right. Stop doing that." Again, it's going to help us all as individuals, and it's also going to help that person in the long run if they don't air some sort of stupid dirty laundry that keeps them from getting hired in the future.

I say this with a certain amount of humility and, even more, from the voice of experience, which I don't like to admit. I've made people angry in the industry. Because of my passion and enthusiasm, I either said things or dug in my heels on projects that hurt people's feelings. It's not the right thing to do, and it has come back to bite me in the tuchus. (I grew up in Chicago, and most of my friends were Jewish, so that's why I use the word tuchus.) If I could go back and talk to my younger self, I'd say, "You thought you were being righteous and fighting the indignation that's out there, but you really weren't. You were being bullheaded and stubborn." I didn't think so at the time, and it wasn't with malicious intent, but I did it, and, to this day, it still comes back. People will look at me and go, "Oh, yeah, Scott. He's *that* guy."

I've tried hard to overcome that, and I've tried hard to change my behavior and make certain I'm not contributing to the negativity that's out there. I'm not the one trashing a former employer. If you read my blog, you know that every time I talk about Busch Gardens, I say there are absolutely no hurt feelings. The same is true with The Vault of Souls. I love that team. The same is true with pretty much every one of my clients, because that's what being a freelancer is all about. You have clients for a while, you have a great time with them, and, when their needs are met, you move on to something else. There's no animosity, and there's no, "This is over, and they screwed me because they didn't give me a permanent job." Well, it was never meant to be a permanent job. My job is a bunch of temporary gigs, and, quite honestly, I love that.

That's why this issue is so important to me and why it's so important to me to say this in the final chapter of this book. It's important to put the word out there and encourage haunters to respect other haunters and treat other people's products with respect—in preparation of, throughout, and after the haunt season—especially in a public forum.

Find Reasons to Compliment Rather than Complain

If you have something negative to say about somebody or you feel they've wronged you in some way—that's probably the most important thing—contact them directly. You may not have the full story, and they may not have the full story. There are a thousand and one different scenarios that this could apply to, but play nice. Certainly, in public, if you're upset with someone, give them the opportunity to share their side of the story—and, by all means, don't publicly trash someone else's haunt.

In all my years in this business, I've done some things I don't think were particularly good. There were a variety of reasons for that, but they just weren't good. In some cases, I just didn't do a good job. What helped me were the people who really cared. I'll give you a perfect example. When The Vault of Souls first opened three years ago, there were some things that weren't well thought out. It was a new project, and it had some aspects that weren't as complete as they should have been. A dear friend of mine came by to experience the event, and, of course, I badly wanted this person to come up to me and say, "I just loved it! I loved every minute of it and thought it was brilliant and wonderful!" They didn't say that, but, because, they were such a trusted friend, they were able to sit down with me and say, "Here's what was missing for me." It's that kind of constructive criticism that helped me make it better and helped me make future projects better. They didn't go into the social forum and rip the event to shreds. On social media, they were quite complimentary and talked about the things they liked. They didn't lie. They talked about the things they liked, and then they came to me privately and said, "I really think this and this and this could have been more." And they were right.

I'm not saying we should blindly love everything, put on our rose-colored glasses, and toss flowers at people—dead roses with eyeballs in the center. I'm not saying we should do that. I'm saying, let's use the things we recognize in other people's work as ways to make their work—and the industry—better. Don't use social media as a whipping post for anyone, about anything. If you have legitimate suggestions, concerns, or even things that plain ol' didn't work, it's okay to go to that person and say, "I saw this, I didn't see this, and I wish I'd seen that." There may be a reason why you didn't see it. In the best-case scenario, they'll look at you and go, "Oh my god! I never thought of that. That's brilliant. That's absolutely brilliant. I'll do that next weekend," or, "I'll do that in my next haunt," or, "I'll do that next year when we remount this."

So, there's very much a time and place for criticism and critique. There's very much a time and place to share your thoughts on people's work. A public forum—and just to be snarky—is not that place.

Everyone and their dog have emailed me with things they didn't like about my past work, and I was completely open to it, because I've had so many people come up to me and praise stuff I've done. I never believe my own press, and I know when something's not perfect. I'm going to keep trying. I think everybody wants to do the best work they possibly can, and I don't think anybody—no matter how strong or weak the end product is—deserves to be ripped to shreds, or even suffer the occasional snarky comment, in a public forum. That's not good for any of us.

Think about Multi-Event Tickets

Next haunt season, I suggest that every haunter go out and support their "competition." I say competition in quotes, because there isn't really competition in the haunt industry. As I mentioned in Chapter 3, if people get scared once and have a good time, they'll want to find another haunt to scare them again. The best thing for any haunted attraction is to have two or three really good haunted attractions in their area. If those haunted attractions are smart, they'll reach out to one another and advertise for each other in their queue lines. If they're really smart, they'll create a multi-event ticket and a punch card. I promise you'll get extra money out of that arrangement. I know there are those people who want to stick with full price and don't want to discount. My feeling is, it's better to have a night where you've got 600 guests and 200 of them are paying a third less than have a night of 400 guests paying full price. Did I do the math right? I think so.

Basically, what I'm saying is, it's better to have more people even if some of them are paying less. This is the mentality of Groupon folks, so why not do it amongst yourselves? Why not take it upon yourselves to band together with this haunt, this haunt, and this haunt? For years, I tried to do this within the theme-park industry, but it was so complex that we couldn't quite make it happen. I urge any haunter reading this to create a multi-haunt ticket. It would benefit haunts and would certainly be great for haunt fans.

Next haunt season, go out and support your "competition," support your fellow haunters, go see their product, have a good night out, and learn stuff from them. If they want your opinion, have the courtesy to share it in a professional manner but not publicly. If somebody else goes to see a haunt and posts a snarky or negative remark on social media, don't add any fuel to that fire. Let it burn out on its own, okay? Let's create a world of haunters supporting haunters.

One of the organizations I'm proud to continue to be a member of is the Haunted Attraction Association. They're an organized way of doing exactly what I'm talking about—elevating the haunt industry in such a way that the people within it treat each other as professionals. If you're a joiner and want to get involved, this is a great organization to get involved with.

Final Words

My passion for the Haunt Industry isn't just in the content. Yes, I have a tendency to be drawn to the beauty found in the dark side of things, but my real inspiration comes from the people who commit hours upon hours to scaring the heck out of their guests. It's the haunters themselves who make the haunt industry so appealing. The information in this book comes from my 20+ years of experience working with incredibly talented people from both corporate and independent haunted attractions. I look forward to what comes next. I'll continue to learn from the dedicated careers of the experts and the wide-eyed optimism of the novices. I'll do my best to keep sharing this information with anyone who'll listen...or read. So, until the next book...Rest in Peace.

Scott can be reached at ScottSwenson.com, AScottInTheDark.com, or through the "A Scott in the Dark" Facebook group.

References

Glickman, Bob. *The Event Brainstormer: Over 800 Creative Concepts & Elements for the Event Professional.* Glickman Productions; 2018.

Swenson, Scott. *Follow the Story: The Foundation of Every Great Attraction.* Philip Hernandez; 2019.

ABOUT THE PUBLISHER

Philip Hernandez is a freelance writer, speaker, producer, and marketer specializing in Seasonal Attractions.

In 2018, Philip became the CEO at Gantom Lighting & Controls, a manufacturer of the world's smallest DMX LED lighting. Gantom is used in every major theme park worldwide to illuminate where other fixtures cannot. Watch Gantom Illuminate: www.gantom.com

Since 2014 Philip has published Seasonal Entertainment Source magazine (SES), a print publication for the seasonal attraction professional. SES ships to readers in over 18 countries. Read articles here: www.seasonalentertainmentsource.com

Philip also operates the Haunted Attraction Network (HAN), an organization connecting the global haunted attraction industry. HAN includes a podcast, articles, videos, and events. Visit HAN here: www.hauntedattractionnetwork.com

Contact Philip for projects here: www.philiplhernandez.com

ABOUT THE AUTHOR

For over 30 years, **Scott Swenson** has been bringing stories to life as a Writer, Director, Producer and Performer. His work in Theme Park, Consumer Events, Live Theater and Television has given him a broad spectrum of experiences. After 21 years working with SeaWorld Parks and Entertainment as the Director of Production, Scott formed *Scott Swenson Creative Development LLC*. Since then he has been writing live shows, creating and implementing themed festivals and developing communication based training classes. Much of Scott's work has focussed on seasonal entertainment. He was co-creator and Creative Leader for the first 15 years of the "Howl-O-Scream" event at Busch Gardens Tampa, during which time he wrote and implemented over 50 haunted houses, shows and scare zones. From 2014 to 2017, he was the Writer and Creative Director for the historically based atmospheric theatre piece, "The Vault of Souls".

Scott has also written and consulted for haunted attractions at Valleyfair Theme Park, SeaWorld Texas and ZooTampa. His most recent projects include "DARK" at Fort Edmonton Park in Edmonton, Alberta Canada and "UNDead in the Water" at The American Victory Ship in Tampa. He is a regular contributor to "Seasonal Entertainment Source" magazine and his podcast, "A Scott in the Dark" continues to grow in popularity. In his "free time" Scott has self published 3 books of dark poetry and prose. In 2017 he was presented a Special Recognition Award from The Haunted Attraction Association for his "…unprecedented investment and support for the haunted attraction industry." He is a sought after panelist and presenter for Entertainment trade shows, especially those focused on haunted attractions and atmospheric theatre.

www.ingramcontent.com/pod-product-compliance
Lightning Source LLC
LaVergne TN
LVHW041542070426
835507LV00011B/878